LEARNING TO LEARN

Strengthening Study Skills and Brain Power

by

Gloria Frender

Incentive Publications, Inc.
Nashville, Tennessee

Cover by Janet March
Edited by Sally Sharpe

ISBN 0-86530-141-7

Acknowledgments and formal notices of copyright for all material under copyright appear on page 240, which is hereby made an extension of the copyright page.

Set a purpose.

Use time wisely.

Concentrate.

Commit yourself to learning.

Evaluate learning styles.

Schedule appropriate study times.

Summarize often.

Fully intend to remember.

Understand assignments.

List priorities.

Set realistic goals.

Think positively.

Use rewards.

Decide to become an independent learner.

You can do it!

Survey textbooks.

Keep up with assignments.

Improve your memory.

Listen actively.

Learn to organize.

Study test-taking strategies.

MEDICINE

I hear and I forget;

I see and I remember;

I do and I understand

Chinese Proverb

For Nylene and Clark, my parents…who gave me self-confidence
and a love for learning
For Dean, Kevin and Kim, my family…who continue to give me
support and love

TABLE OF CONTENTS

READING SKILLS

MEMORY

TEST-TAKING SKILLS

ETC.

LEARNING HOW TO LEARN is one of the most valuable tools available to help students achieve success in school and life. The "brain power" one applies to any task is critical. In order for students to improve their performance in school, they must understand all there is to gain from improvement, and they must be committed to actively pursuing their goals. Once an individual realizes success and the wonderful feelings of self-confidence and pride that follow, the task of learning becomes easier. This book contains the ideas, suggestions and strategies to help students achieve that success.

LEARNING HOW TO LEARN is intended for students, teachers, parents and anyone who wants a hands-on guide and reference for "learning how to learn." This book is not a book to read; it is a book to use, to write in and to tear apart. It is a book filled with practical hints, methods, tips, procedures, resources and tools that will help students succeed in school. Care has been taken to omit any "educational jargon" and to present the material in a straightforward manner.

The format of organized step-by-step procedures has been broken down into manageable blocks that apply across all content areas. Throughout the book the main concepts are stressed with a positive attitude, a feeling of accomplishment and self-worth, and a sense of humor.

What sets this book apart from other study skills books is the construction of every concept — a format that allows the "user" to get right to the heart of the matter in a simplified manner. Now good ideas are easy to find, digest and put to immediate use.

LEARNING STYLES

Focus On
Learning Styles

1. Know how you learn.

2. Combine HOW and WHY with WHAT you learn.

3. Be aware of the time and environment where you learn best.

4. Apply various learning activities to meet your needs.

5. Utilize all your senses in learning anything.

6. Apply how you learn to all new situations.

7. Be flexible in your thinking and learning.

8. Intentionally decide which modality to use.

9. Analyze your teacher's teaching style and use appropriate learning strategies.

10. Creatively adapt materials to best fit your learning strengths.

LEARNING STYLES & YOU

You are what you are! Each individual naturally functions and learns in a particular manner. Although your brain usually functions as a "whole," it actually is divided into two hemispheres. Both hemispheres act and react, think and process, and solve problems in very specific ways. Each is quite different from the other, and one is usually dominant. The best "brain power" is a result of both hemispheres integrating with almost equal balance.

You learn primarily through three basic modalities which use your senses: visual (seeing), auditory (hearing), and kinesthetic (feeling, doing). Just like left or right hemisphere brain dominance, one modality is usually predominant.

In order to learn "how to learn," it is very important to learn how you presently take in and process information. Knowing the strengths and weaknesses of your individual learning style will allow you to make adjustments so that you may reach your fullest potential in whatever you wish to do or learn. Assessing your learning style is the first step toward achieving maximum use of your "brain power."

Self-assessments in the areas of brain ability and modality strengths, as well as specific attributes of each, may be found on pages 17-20. This information will be invaluable to you as you continue your journey toward more effective and efficient learning.

LEFT/RIGHT BRAIN SELF-ASSESSMENT

Read the following left and right brain characteristics and circle the most appropriate answers. The scoring table at the end of the list will help you determine your "dominance." You may find that you are fairly balanced between the two hemispheres.

1. I have no trouble making decisions about the correct thing to do.

2. I see problems or pictures as a whole rather than in parts or details.

3. I follow written directions best and prefer to write and talk.

4. I often think of many things at once rather than thinking through one idea at a time.

5. I'm usually aware of the time.

6. When I'm introduced to someone for the first time, I pay particular attention to the person's face. I later forget the person's name, but I remember his or her face.

7. I attack most problem-solving activities analytically and logically.

8. When comparing things, I usually look for ways they are alike rather than ways they are different.

9. I'd rather take a true/false, multiple-choice or matching test than an essay test.

10. Most often, I use my imagination and I think in an abstract manner.

11. If I have a problem, I break it down into smaller, more manageable parts in order to arrive at a solution.

12. I seem to learn best if I can observe a demonstration or read the directions.

13. Generally, I like to be in control of a situation and I do not like to take too many risks.

14. I like assignments that are open-ended rather than more structured assignments.

15. I learn best by seeing and hearing.

16. I learn best by touching or doing.

17. I usually think in concrete patterns and solve problems with a step-by-step approach.

18. If I try to remember information, I generally picture it in my mind.

19. Although I sometimes get upset, I am a rational person.

20. I don't mind trying anything once; I take risks when it is necessary.

21. Sometimes I talk to myself in order to think or learn something.

22. I can let my feelings "go." I am considered to be somewhat emotional.

23. I solve problems on an intellectual basis rather than an intuitive one.

24. People have told me that I'm creative.

25. I prefer to think of one thing at a time.

26. I like to act in a spontaneous manner.

27. I prefer to plan things and know what's going to happen ahead of time.

28. I can easily remember melodies and tunes.

29. I am usually in control of my feelings.

30. I do well in geometry and geography.

31. I usually can recall information I need quickly and easily.

32. I enjoy reading and writing poetry; it comes to me easily.

33. I can really concentrate when I want to.

34. When I work in a group, I can "feel" the moods of others.

35. I understand mathematical concepts.

36. When solving problems or taking tests, I rely on one idea leading to another in order to come to a conclusion.

37. I can learn new vocabulary words easily.

38. When I plan a party, I "hang loose" rather than plan all of the details.

39. I usually can learn easily from any teacher.

40. In class I'm generally aware of what everyone is doing.

41. I notice and remember details.

42. I can easily see the whole picture when only a few puzzle pieces are in place.

43. I don't mind practicing something repeatedly in order to master it.

44. I communicate best with someone "in person" rather than on the phone.

45. I can remember jokes and punch lines.

46. I have trouble concentrating when I know I should.

47. I can write directions in a clear and logical manner.

48. I sometimes rely on my intuition when making decisions.

49. I basically have a day-to-day routine.

50. I sometimes can remember things according to where I "saw" them on the page.

SCORING TABLE		
_____ even numbers circled	=	RIGHT BRAIN ABILITY
_____ odd numbers circled	=	LEFT BRAIN ABILITY

- Remember, this inventory is only an informal indication of which hemisphere is probably dominant for you. Both sides work together and cannot be totally separated.

LEFT/RIGHT BRAIN DOMINANCE CHARACTERISTICS

<u>LEFT</u>

- sequential
- intellectual
- structure/planned
- controls feelings
- analytical
- logical
- remembers names
- rational
- solves problems by breaking them apart
- time-oriented
- auditory/visual learner
- prefers to write and talk
- follows spoken directions
- talks to think and learn
- prefers T/F, multiple-choice and matching tests
- takes few risks (with control)
- looks for the differences
- controls right side of body
- thinks mathematically
- thinks concretely
- language
- thinks of one thing at a time

<u>RIGHT</u>

- holistic
- intuitive
- spontaneous
- lets feelings go
- creative/responsive
- more abstract
- remembers faces
- more likely to act on emotions
- solves problems by looking at the whole
- spatially oriented
- kinesthetic learner
- prefers to draw and handle objects
- follows written or demonstrated directions
- "pictures" things to think and learn
- prefers essay tests
- takes more risks (less control)
- looks for similar qualities
- controls left side of body
- musical abilities
- emotional
- thinks simultaneously

A *learning modality* is a way of using sensory information to learn. Basically, there are three modalities you use to process material into your memory. They are as follows:

- visual   – learn from seeing
- auditory   – learn from hearing
- kinesthetic – learn from touching, doing, moving

Generally, everyone has one predominant modality. However, many people have a "balance" between two or even all three senses. It is very important to know your primary sense of learning so that you will know how to approach learning and how to apply certain methods that will aid you the most.

First, complete the self-assessment on pages 22-24 to find out what your strongest modality is. Then, refer to the chart of suggested aids for learning modalities on page 26 for specific hints and methods you can use to increase your learning power.

SELF-ASSESSMENT OF MODALITY STRENGTHS

Read each question or statement and circle the most appropriate answer. Some will be difficult to answer, but try to respond according to how you would react most often.

1. **You usually remember more from a class lecture when:**
   a. you do not take notes but listen very closely
   b. you sit near the front of the room and watch the speaker
   c. you take notes (whether or not you look at them again)

2. **You usually solve problems by:**
   a. talking to yourself or a friend
   b. using an organized, systematic approach with lists, schedules, etc.
   c. walking, pacing or some other physical activity

3. **You remember phone numbers (when you can't write them down) by:**
   a. repeating the numbers orally
   b. "seeing" or "visualizing" the numbers in your mind
   c. "writing" the numbers with your finger on a table or wall

4. **You find it easiest to learn something new by:**
   a. listening to someone explain how to do it
   b. watching a demonstration of how to do it
   c. trying it yourself

5. **You remember most clearly from a movie:**
   a. what the characters said, background noises and music
   b. the setting, scenery and costumes
   c. the feelings you experienced during the movie

6. **When you go to the grocery store, you:**
   a. silently or orally repeat the grocery list
   b. walk up and down the aisles to see what you need
   c. usually remember what you need from the list you left at home

continued

7. **You are trying to remember something and so you:**
    a. try to see it happen in your mind
    b. hear in your mind what was said or the noises that occurred
    c. feel the way "it" reacted with your emotions

8. **You learn a foreign language best by:**
    a. listening to records or tapes
    b. writing and using workbooks
    c. attending a class in which you read and write

9. **You are confused about the correct spelling of a word and so you:**
    a. sound it out
    b. try to "see" the word in your mind
    c. write the word several different ways and choose the one that looks right

10. **You enjoy reading most when you can read:**
    a. dialogue between characters
    b. descriptive passages that allow you to create mental pictures
    c. stories with a lot of action in the beginning (because you have a hard time sitting still)

11. **You usually remember people you have met by their:**
    a. names (you forget faces)
    b. faces (you forget names)
    c. mannerisms, motions, etc.

12. **You are distracted most by:**
    a. noises
    b. people
    c. environment (temperature, comfort of furniture, etc.)

continued

13. You usually dress:
   a. fairly well (but clothes are not very important to you)
   b. neatly (in a particular style)
   c. comfortably (so you can move easily)

14. You can't do anything physical and you can't read, so you choose to:
   a. talk with a friend
   b. watch T V or look out a window
   c. move slightly in your chair or bed

SCORING

1. Count the total number of responses for each letter and write them below.

   a. _____ auditory   (learn best by hearing)

   b. _____ visual   (learn best by seeing)

   c. _____ kinesthetic   (learn best by touching, doing, moving)

2. Notice if one modality is significantly higher or lower, or if any two modalities are close in number.

3. Were the results as you expected them to be? Is that the way you see yourself?

CHARACTERISTICS OF LEARNING STYLES

Three of your five senses are primarily used in learning, storing, remembering and recalling information. Your eyes, ears and sense of touch play essential roles in the way you communicate, perceive reality and relate to others. Because you learn from and communicate best with someone who shares your dominant modality, it is a great advantage for you to know the characteristics of visual, auditory and kinesthetic learning styles and to be able to identify them in others.

VISUAL	AUDITORY	KINESTHETIC
mind sometimes strays during verbal activities	talks to self aloud	likes physical rewards
observes rather than talks or acts	enjoys talking	in motion most of the time
organized in approach to tasks	easily distracted	likes to touch people when talking to them
likes to read	has more difficulty with written directions	taps pencil or foot while studying
usually a good speller	likes to be read to	enjoys doing activities
memorizes by seeing graphics & pictures	memorizes by steps in a sequence	reading is not a priority
not too distractible	enjoys music	poor speller
finds verbal instructions difficult	whispers to self while reading	likes to solve problems by physically working through them
has good handwriting	remembers faces	will try new things
remembers faces	easily distracted by noises	outgoing by nature; expresses emotions through physical means
uses advanced planning	hums or sings	uses hands while talking
doodles	outgoing by nature	dresses for comfort
quiet by nature	enjoys listening activities	enjoys handling objects
meticulous, neat in appearance		
notices details		

- Students who have equal modality preferences are more flexible learners and are already using many studying techniques rather than just a few.

SUGGESTED AIDS FOR LEARNING MODALITIES

Use these aids to sharpen your particular dominant learning modality or to strengthen a weaker one. Try to be aware of the different activities you do daily to help all three of your modalities.

VISUAL	AUDITORY	KINESTHETIC
use guided imagery	use tapes	pace/walk as you study
form pictures in your mind	watch T V	physically "do it"
take notes	listen to music	practice by repeated motion
see parts of words	speak/listen to speakers	breathe slowly
use "cue" words	make up rhymes/poems	role play
use notebooks	read aloud	exercise
use color codes	talk to yourself	dance
use study cards	repeat things orally	write
use photographic pictures	use rhythmic sounds	write on surfaces with finger
watch T V	have discussions	take notes
watch filmstrips	listen carefully	associate feelings with concept/information
watch movies	use oral directions	write lists repeatedly
use charts, graphs	sound out words	stretch/move in chair
use maps	use theater	watch lips move in front of a mirror
demonstrate	say words in syllables	use mnemonics (word links, rhymes, poems, lyrics), refer to "Memory Chapter"
draw/use drawings	use mnemonics (word links, rhymes, poems, lyrics), refer to "Memory Chapter"	
use exhibits		
watch lips move in front of a mirror		
use mnemonics (acronyms, visual chains, mind maps, acrostics, hook-ups), refer to "Memory Chapter"		

ENVIRONMENTS FOR BETTER LEARNING

Be aware of the environment in which you learn best. Consider the following alternatives and make a conscious effort to use those environments that allow you to learn most efficiently and effectively. If you can become more knowledgeable about your environment while you study, you soon will learn to repeat these conditions to achieve your maximum study potential!

	Under what conditions do you study best?
	silence, background music, low noise or noisy sounds
	bright, medium or low light
	sitting up straight at a desk or relaxing on the bed or floor
	in the early morning, afternoon, evening or late at night
	being still or moving around

SOME FACTS ON LEARNING STYLES

- Once you understand your learning style, you are more likely to know how to meet your own needs.

- Students can accurately predict their learning modalities.

- Students who are matched with teachers of the same learning style learn best. Students who can accurately predict their teachers' learning/teaching styles learn better than students who cannot make this prediction.

- A student's learning style is the same no matter what the subject area.

- Students score higher on tests when they are tested in the environments best suited to their personal learning styles — bright versus dim lighting, silence versus sound, etc.

- Persistent and responsible students achieve higher grades and score higher on tests.

- A key to quick learning and memory is to change the information to be learned into the form that the brain can learn most easily.

- The more a student can utilize learning through the combination of visual, auditory and kinesthetic modalities, the more permanent the information will become.

SCIENCE

TIME MANAGEMENT & ORGANIZATION SKILLS

FOCUS ON TIME MANAGEMENT AND ORGANIZATION

1. Intend to accomplish your goal in a reasonable amount of time.

2. Be realistic in eliminating excuses; reward yourself for positive behavior.

3. Break up long-term assignments into reasonable units.

4. Set priorities carefully in order to save time.

5. Keep organized.

6. Make daily "to-do" lists.

7. Make realistic schedules and follow them.

8. Use quality study time – not quantity study time.

9. Make time to warm up your mind and review your knowledge.

10. Always ask yourself if that was the best use of your time.

TIME MANAGEMENT

Time plays a major role in every enterprise on earth. Time schedules form a foundation for every kind of work you do.

Young people are naturally less conscious of time than people who have lived longer. During a child's early years, parents help to watch the clock and manage the child's time. The child begins to think of time as something invisible, controlled by his or her parents, that regulates what he or she can do. As the child grows up and begins to think about gaining independence, he or she often imagines that this new freedom means no longer having to live by time rules.

The first and easiest way for a young person to gain more freedom is to prove his or her skill in handling time. When an individual can manage a time schedule successfully, without prodding or reminders from parents, he or she is well on the way to self-reliance. People learn to trust such an individual. Even more importantly, the individual learns to trust himself or herself.

Setting up a time schedule and making it work is a tough assignment that requires commitment and perseverance. There are countless pitfalls in planning activities and assignments in terms of weeks, days and hours. There are good reasons for "putting things off," and many mistakes often are made in determining how much actually can be done in a certain amount of time.

Discovering these problems is the first step toward progress — not a sign of failure. The second step is to revise the schedule to better fit the need. Make this second revision more realistic, but set the goal a little beyond what you think will work. Again, this step will take more patience and persistence, but it will produce a more satisfactory system. The end result will be a more efficient and successful habit which subsequently gives you more time to spend as you wish!

Just how well do you study? Have you thought seriously about *how, when, where* and *why* you study? Knowing the answers to these questions can help you form some very important habits or improve the habits you already practice.

If you don't know the answers to these questions or you aren't sure if you're using time efficiently, perhaps some of these questions will help you think about what you need to do to improve.

Take a few minutes to answer the questions on the "Study Habits Inventory" (page 34). You may find out some new things about yourself!

STUDY HABITS INVENTORY

	Hardly Ever	Sometimes	Most Always
1. Do you intend to study, concentrate and learn?	_____	_____	_____
2. Do you follow a daily written schedule?	_____	_____	_____
3. Do you have a regular place to work and study?	_____	_____	_____
4. Is it well-equipped, well-lighted and comfortable?	_____	_____	_____
5. Do you keep track of home-work assignments in a book?	_____	_____	_____
6. Do you keep a long-term schedule or calendar of tests, projects and reports?	_____	_____	_____
7. Do you plan weekly reviews?	_____	_____	_____
8. Do you take effective class notes?	_____	_____	_____
9. Do you keep a notebook for every subject?	_____	_____	_____
10. Are you organized?	_____	_____	_____
11. Do you have a note-taking system?	_____	_____	_____
12. Do you edit your notes?	_____	_____	_____

From *Senior High Study Skills Booklet*, Jefferson County Schools, Colorado, © 1983. Used by permission.

	Hardly Ever	Sometimes	Most Always
13. Do you compile study sheets for tests?	_____	_____	_____
14. Do you know how you learn best?	_____	_____	_____
15. Do you study with friends?	_____	_____	_____
16. Do you listen well in class?	_____	_____	_____
17. Do you know what distracts you?	_____	_____	_____
18. Do you look up new words?	_____	_____	_____
19. Do you keep track of new words you learn?	_____	_____	_____
20. Do you use the glossary?	_____	_____	_____
21. Do you have a study system for textbooks?	_____	_____	_____
22. Do you outline reading assignments?	_____	_____	_____
23. Do you skim assignments before reading them?	_____	_____	_____
24. Do you read tables, charts and graphs?	_____	_____	_____
25. Do you have a private shorthand system for taking notes?	_____	_____	_____
26. Do you organize papers before you write?	_____	_____	_____

	Hardly Ever	Sometimes	Most Always
27. Do you write a first draft?	_____	_____	_____
28. Do you proofread for spelling and punctuation errors?	_____	_____	_____
29. Do you study effectively?	_____	_____	_____
30. Do you learn in school?	_____	_____	_____
31. Do you get enough sleep every night?	_____	_____	_____
32. Do you exercise regularly?	_____	_____	_____
33. Do you study at the same time each day?	_____	_____	_____
34. Do you make good use of your mind?	_____	_____	_____
35. Do you try to improve your study habits?	_____	_____	_____
36. Do you space your study periods over several days?	_____	_____	_____
37. Do you keep up-to-date with your studies?	_____	_____	_____
38. Do you review often?	_____	_____	_____

If you find yourself saying these things, then perhaps you better ask yourself these questions!

"I'm here and that's enough."

Ask yourself   "Since I'm not putting out any effort, should I expect anything in return?"

"I just don't have the time."

Ask yourself   "Is studying really a priority? How many things do I find to do that don't have to be done, at least right now?"

"Well, I'll start tomorrow."

Ask yourself   "How many times have I said that? Is that a convenient excuse? What will I say tomorrow?"

"I can't!"

Ask yourself   "How many ways/methods have I tried? How many times have I tried? Have I tried to get help?"

"I don't need to study."

Ask yourself   "Why do I think this? What is my grade in the class?"

"I'm just too tired."

Ask yourself   "Would I be this tired if I had the choice to do something else? How much sleep did I get last night?"

"It's boring."

Ask yourself   "What do I expect to get out of this? How have I tried to relate the information to my life? Do I really need the information?"

"It's just too much for me, so why start now?"

Ask yourself   "Is there anything I can realistically accomplish now? Why am I in this mess? When should I have started the assignment?"

Now, tell yourself "I WILL...AND I CAN!"

TOOLS FOR STUDY

1. **Reference Books**
   - dictionary
   - thesaurus
   - English handbook (Suggestion: *Writers Inc.* by Sebranek, Meyer, & Kemper. © 1989 by The Write Source.)
   - atlas
   - almanac

2. **Utensils**
   - room light and desk lamp
   - pens (erasable?)
   - pencils/erasers
   - colored pens/pencils
   - colored highlighters/underliners
   - template (great for creating graphic organizers)
   - ruler
   - compass
   - scissors
   - stapler
   - paper clips
   - tape
   - rubber cement
   - calculator
   - timer or clock

3. **Paper**
   - large monthly planner/calendar
   - notebooks (one for each subject)
   - scratch tablets/paper
   - index cards (3 x 5, 4 x 6 or 5 x 8)
   - colored typing paper (great for coding study sheets)

4. **Miscellaneous**
   - bulletin board
   - cassette tape/recorder
   - facial tissues

Have you tried using an assignment sheet for each of your classes?

1. Purchase an assignment notebook that you use for assignments only.
2. Use one assignment sheet (page 41) for each class.
3. Take the assignment sheet/notebook with you to every class.
4. Write each assignment on the assignment sheet in the proper space.
5. Next to each assignment, write the following:
    *   estimated time required to complete the assignment
    *   date assignment is due
    *   special materials needed

Have you tried using 3 x 5 index cards for assignments?

1. Use one 3 x 5 index card for each assignment.
2. Write the specific assignment.
3. Note the estimated time required to complete the assignment.
4. Note the date the assignment is due.
5. Keep these cards in a packet and refer to them often.

From *Senior High Study Skills Booklet*, Jefferson County Schools, Colorado, © 1983. Used by permission.
© 1990 by Incentive Publications, Inc., Nashville, TN.

Have you tried keeping a daily "to-do" list?

1. Use index cards of any size.
2. Write what you want to do and must accomplish each day on an index card.
3. Assign a priority number for each of the items on the card.
4. Cross off each item as you complete the task. This action will give you a sense of accomplishment!
5. Keep the index card with you throughout the day and refer to it often.

From *Senior High Study Skills Booklet*, Jefferson County Schools, Colorado, © 1983. Used by permission.

Other Helpful Hints:

- Post a note to yourself reminding you to take your assignment notebook/sheet home from school (see "Before You Leave School Checklist," page 51).

- Be sure you understand the full assignment before leaving class. If you have any questions, ask the teacher.

ASSIGNMENT SHEET

WEEK OF _____

	ASSIGNMENT	DUE DATE	ESTIMATED TIME	MATERIALS NEEDED	DONE
THIS WEEK					
LATER					

	MATERIAL TESTED	DATE	TYPE OF TEST	SPECIAL NOTES	
EXAMS					

ORGANIZING A NOTEBOOK

A well-organized and useful notebook is a definite aid to maintaining good study habits and achieving better grades. A single folder filled with the necessary papers and schedules can do much to "head off" last-minute panic!

Consider including the following in your notebook:

- class requirement sheets
- table of contents (Be sure to leave room for additional items to be added throughout the course.)
- assignment sheets
- monthly calendar
- class notes
- graphic organizers
- handouts
- list of classmates and their phone numbers
- names and phone numbers of study group members
- assignments underway as well as past assignments
- notes from outside reading or research, lab notes, etc.
- returned tests
- study skills information sheets and/or guides
- your name, address and phone number
- reports or projects

You might want to section off different categories (class notes, reading assignments, study sheets, etc.) with colored dividers and tabs. It's handy to have the assignment sheet on the inside cover for quick reference. Look for a place to put an extra pencil or pen.

Unless a specific format or type of notebook is required by your teacher, choose one that best fits your organizational style. Make it work for you — and keep it organized!

What To Do If You Missed An Assignment

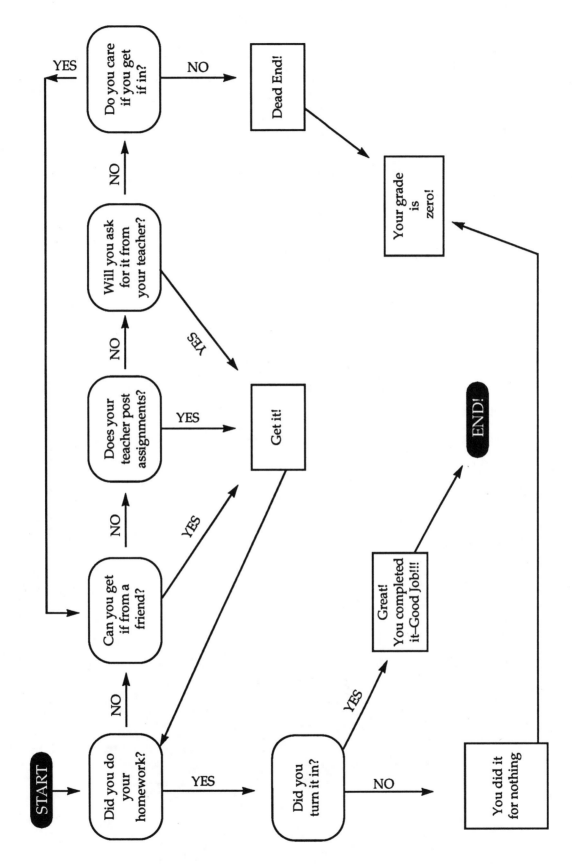

From *The Campus Cache: A Cookbook For Study Skills*, The CMU Junior League, Cherry Creek School District, © 1982. Used by permission.
© 1990 by Incentive Publications, Inc., Nashville, TN.

To-Do List

POINTS TO CONSIDER WHEN CREATING A "TO-DO" LIST:

- prepare each evening for the next day
- keep this list with you
- be realistic — there are only 24 hours in a day
- cross off items as you do them (this gives you immediate satisfaction and it shows your progress)
- add new items whenever you think of them
- use a coding system to set priorities
- ask yourself these questions when setting priorities:

    What must be done by tomorrow?

    How can I best use my time at this point in the day?

- use a notebook and index cards
- put items left over from today's list on tomorrow's list
- realistically estimate the amount of time needed to complete each task — then add one more
- give yourself a reward for completing every task on your "to-do" list

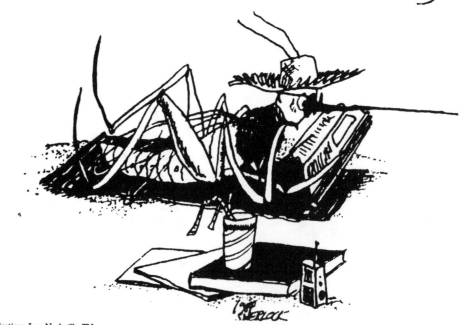

My "To-Do" List

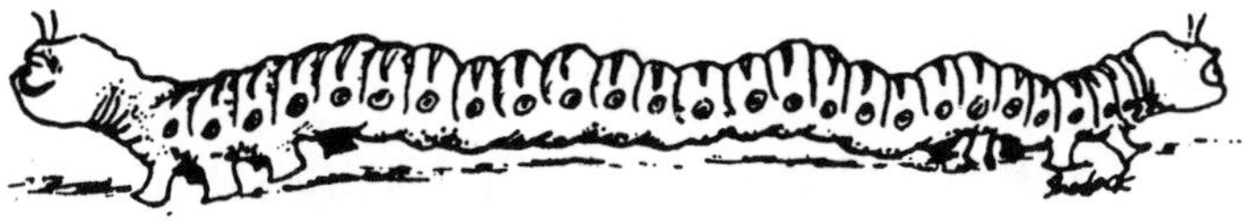

Priority Date ________________

______ ______________________________

______ ______________________________

______ ______________________________

______ ______________________________

______ ______________________________

______ ______________________________

______ ______________________________

______ ______________________________

______ ______________________________

______ ______________________________

Notes To Myself:

SCHEDULES: THE BACKBONE OF GOOD STUDY HABITS

I. **ANALYZE HOW YOU CURRENTLY USE YOUR TIME.**

   A. **Carefully consider.**
   1. When and where do you study?
   2. How often do you study?
   3. How much time do you waste and how much time do you spend wisely?
   4. What is the quality of your study time?
   5. What "excuses" do you use regularly?
   6. What are your priorities?

II. **LEARN HOW TO MAKE A SCHEDULE.**

   A. **Make a list of daily activities and realistically estimate the amount of time required to complete each.**
   1. Consider priorities in this order:
      a. In-class time
      b. Work hours
      c. Meals
      d. Sleep
      e. Classes outside school
      f. Family activities
      g. Study block time (begin with at least one hour daily)
      h. Recreation time

   B. **Using one of the schedules provided (pages 49 and 50) write each activity in the appropriate space.**
   1. Consider these hints before you begin:
      a. Make the schedule somewhat flexible.
         1. Don't schedule every hour of every day.
         2. Leave room for the unexpected.
         3. Leave room for change, but only make a change for a good reason.
      b. Write legibly.
      c. Be realistic — you know yourself best.

Schedules: The Backbone of Good Study Habits

continued

III. POST SCHEDULES/ASSIGNMENTS/LISTS.

    A. **Keep a calendar:**
        1. In a notebook
        2. Inside your locker door
        3. On a bulletin board or wall in your room (great visual reinforcement)

    B. **Post time schedules of home activities:**
        1. On the refrigerator door
        2. On a family bulletin board
        3. Include the following:
           a. Study blocks for all family members
           b. Family activities
           c. Special events

    C. **Make and post daily "to-do" lists.**

IV. HINTS FOR SUCCESSFUL SCHEDULES:

    A. **Try using your schedule for one week before making changes.**

    B. **Become familiar with your schedule and make the schedule a habit.**

    C. **Post it so that you will see it several times each day.**

    D. **Carry it with you for easy reference.**

    E. **Remember to be flexible and to change something only if there is a good reason.**

SETTING PRIORITIES

Setting priorities can be difficult. Compromises are sometimes necessary. Use this sheet to "sort out" any conflicts and to selectively choose items from each column in a realistic and conscientious manner. This can be a helpful activity when creating a weekly/monthly schedule, daily "to-do" list, and planning a block of time for study. Brainstorm and list any ideas that pop into your head. Then, review each item and number it according to the priorities of time and importance. Have fun with it!

Things I Want To Do   **Things I Should Do**

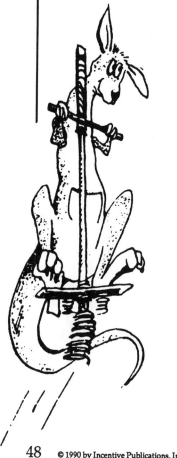

Monthly Assignment Schedule

Month _____

Monday	Tuesday	Wednesday	Thursday	Friday

Classes:

DAILY SCHEDULE

	Monday	Tuesday	Wednesday	Thursday	Friday	Saturday	Sunday
5:00							
6:00							
7:00							
8:00							
9:00							
10:00							
11:00							
12:00							
1:00							
2:00							
3:00							
4:00							
5:00							
6:00							
7:00							
8:00							
9:00							
10:00							
11:00							
12:00							

BEFORE YOU LEAVE SCHOOL CHECKLIST

	Assignment sheet is complete for each class/subject.
	Understand all assignments and due dates.
	Gather all necessary books, notebooks, materials and supplies.
	Stop by the library/media center if necessary.
	Talk to or see any necessary persons.
	Review "to-do" list.

Post this checklist in your locker or on the inside cover of the notebook you use for your last class of the day. This will help you avoid the "I forgot" syndrome!

CAUSES OF POOR CONCENTRATION

CONCENTRATION is the ability to control your attention.

- distracting noises

- your body "condition"

- boredom

- daydreaming

- hunger

- worry

- dislike of subject

- wrong "time" of day

- T V

- overwhelming feeling about the task or assignment

- lack of commitment

- constant interruptions

- poor attention span

- indecision to study

- lack of sleep

- poor diet

GOOD HABITS FOR BETTER CONCENTRATION:

1. **Intend to study and learn.**

2. **Become interested in the subject.**
   - Look for points of view.
   - Question and dare to disagree.
   - Predict outcome.
   - See connections/relations within the information.

3. **Know yourself.**
   - Take advantage of your learning style and modality.
   - Use your positive aspects.

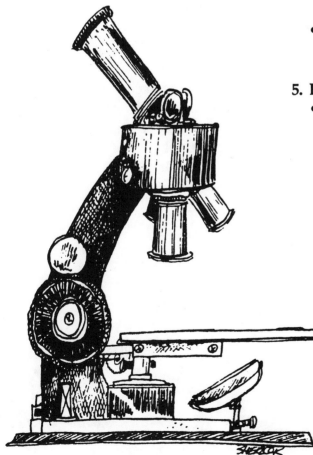

4. **Set clear and realistic goals.**
   - Know what you are supposed to learn.
   - Concentrate on the focus of the material/information.
   - Briefly outline tasks to be completed.

5. **Exclude distractions.**
   - Keep a "distractions list" and continually try to reduce it. (We are often distracted by the same things again and again, but we usually are unaware of these things.)

6. **Use a timer to remind you that a certain amount of time has passed.**
   - Intend to concentrate and accomplish a certain amount of learning in a specific amount of time.

7. **Eliminate daydreaming from study time!**
   - Make a tic/check mark on a piece of paper each time you catch yourself daydreaming.
   - Continually try to reduce the number of tic marks from one study block to the next.

8. **Vary your routine within the study block.**
   - Change subjects if you become bored.
   - Take a 5-10 minute break for every 30-45 minute period of concentration.
   - Allow 15-20 minutes for your brain to refocus before beginning new material.

9. **Summarize more often.**
   - Talk to yourself as if you're teaching someone the information.
   - Talk to someone who is interested in the subject.

10. **Reward yourself for focused, sustained concentration.**
    - Start with reasonable expectations and short blocks of concentration.
    - Continually attempt to lengthen the duration of study blocks.
    - Be positive!
    - Tell yourself, "That's a job well-done!"

I. **IDENTIFY YOUR PRIORITIES AND SET ASIDE AMPLE TIME IN YOUR SCHEDULE TO MEET THESE PRIORITIES.**

   A. **Consider the following:**
      1. After-school activities
      2. Lessons
      3. Club meetings
      4. Homework
      5. Friends

   B. **Plan to space blocks of study time over several days on long-range assignments.**
      1. Helps you retain new knowledge.
      2. Helps to make learning more permanent.
      3. Gives you time to think about and change written assignments.

   C. **Realistically plan your time.**
      1. One regular block of time each day is best for making studying a habit.
      2. Estimate completion time of assignments.
         a. Read/write one page and then multiply by the total number of pages.
         b. Consider regular ongoing assignments per class.

   D. **Do not try to study if you are:**
      1. Hungry
      2. Tired
      3. Too cold/hot
      4. Too comfortable/ uncomfortable
      5. Worried or upset
      6. Too distracted
      7. Sick

II. KNOW YOURSELF.

A. Know *when* you study best:
1. Are you a morning or night person?
2. When are you most productive, awake and alert?
3. Do you let everyone know when it is your time to study so that you will not be disturbed?
4. Have you formed a habit of studying the same time each day?

B. Know *where* you study best.
1. Consider these distractions:
   a. T.V.
   b. Talking
   c. Windows (activity outside the windows)
   d. Music (some kinds of music are distracting to some people whereas other kinds are not)
   e. particular objects on a desk/table
   f. people walking by
2. Your own bedroom is probably the best place to study.

C. Know *why* you are studying:
1. Why do you need this knowledge/information?
2. How is it relevant to you and what you want to do with it?

D. Know your learning style:
1. Left/right brain dominance (refer to "Learning Styles" chapter)
2. Visual/auditory/kinesthetic learning modalities
3. Do you study best alone or with others?

III. SELECT A SPECIAL STUDY PLACE.

A. Environment:
1. Comfortable, but not too comfortable (to keep you from falling asleep)
2. Ventilated
3. Quiet
4. Away from things that distract you
5. Well-lighted

B. Use the same place as often as possible.
1. Make it a habit.
2. Keep study tools on hand.

READY ... SET ... STUDY!

I. **GATHER ALL MATERIALS NEEDED.**

   A. Reference books

   B. Writing tools

   C. Tests

   D. Class notes

   E. Folders, notebooks, etc.

   F. Assignment sheet

   G. Refer to "Tools For Study" (page 38)

II. **SET YOUR MIND TO STUDY.**

   A. **Intend to have focused, effective study time.**
   B. **Set realistic goals/purposes to be met during the study session.**
     1. Strive for quality as well as quantity.
     2. Try to make short and intermediate goals within the time block.

   C. **Become actively involved.**
     1. Continually ask yourself questions about the material.
     2. Remind yourself to review material often.

III. **SET PRIORITIES FOR ASSIGNMENTS.**

   A. **Create a "to-do" list for each study block and assign a priority for each assignment to be completed.**

B. Map out a time line.
  1. For long-range assignments:
    a. Work backwards from due dates.
    b. Consider the following:
      1. Length of assignment
      2. Difficulty of book to be read
      3. Number of questions to be answered
      4. Presentation mode: handwriting or typing
  2. Set intermediate goals by a certain date.
    a. Short-range "chunks" of work are easier to focus upon and handle.
    b. Congratulate yourself for completing each intermediate goal.
  3. Divide time among the subjects.
    a. Study the hardest thing first, when your mind is fresh.
    b. Leave routine and less difficult tasks for last.
      1. Recopying papers
      2. Alphabetizing
      3. Organizing reports
      4. Creating the table of contents
  4. Allow time blocks to be spaced over several hours or days.
    a. This allows material to be "soaked into the subconscious."
    b. Reflective time is necessary.
    c. This is much better for proofreading material.

IV. WARM UP YOUR BRAIN.

A. Take 1-5 minutes to warm up your mind.
B. Be sure you understand the assignment/requirements for the subject.

  1. Ask yourself:
    a. What do I already know about this?
    b. What am I trying to learn from this material?
    c. What am I to know by the end of this study block?

C. Review familiar material first.
1. Titles/subtitles
2. Boldface type/italics
3. Vocabulary words
4. Review questions
5. Class notes/teacher handouts

D. Apply knowledge of how you learn to warm up and study.
1. Use available materials during the study block to make the best use of your learning style.
   a. Write things (repeatedly, if necessary)
      1. Vocabulary words
      2. Lists
      3. Definitions
      4. Diagrams/charts
   b. Make a tape of things to remember/memorize.
   c. Write important information on 3 x 5 cards and post the cards in your room.
2. Learn new study skills that work for you.

V. TAKE A BREAK.

A. Take a 5-10 minute break for every 30-45 minute study period.
1. Do something physical.
   a. Get something to eat.
   b. Walk.
   c. Call a friend.

B. Take a short break when switching subjects/topics.

WHEN YOU FINISH AN ASSIGNMENT:

REVIEW
- Briefly review as a summary activity.
  - Skim/scan texts, notes and handouts.
  - Talk to yourself.
  - Recreate mind maps or other graphic organizers.
  - In your mind, try to explain it to someone else.
- Talk about it with a friend/classmate/parent.
- Review again within 24 hours.

OVERLEARN
- Form a study group.
- Keep a running list of vocabulary words.
- Reread the assignment and your homework to be sure you have completed what was expected.
- Make up test questions about what you have learned.
- Repeat the review steps.

EVALUATE
- Is your homework in the correct format, is it organized, and is it easy to read?
- Is this your best effort?
- Did you learn what you set out to learn?
- Do you really know the information for which you will be held responsible?
  - Is there a way you can improve?
  - Can you relate the material to show that you know it?

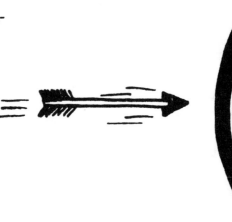

The "Study Prescription Work-sheet" (page 63) is designed to be an activity which allows you to "trouble-shoot" and "target" troublesome classes, subjects and materials and, more importantly, match each with a solution. Review this chapter (or any others) for appropriate strategies, methods, hints and approaches to basic skills in order to solve the "trouble" areas. Remember, for every problem there is a solution. It just may be that the process of finding the right solution is a bit frustrating at times. Be persistent and confident. Don't forget to seek help if you need it.

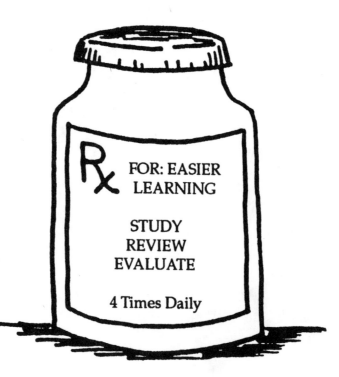

STUDY PRESCRIPTION WORKSHEET

LIST CLASSES HERE	LIST PROBLEMS WITH STUDYING FOR EACH CLASS HERE	LIST SOLUTIONS & STUDY STRATEGIES FOR EACH CLASS HERE	RESULTS	REWARDS

GREAT STUDY TIPS

- Allow time for information to "soak in."

- Too many new ideas at one time are confusing.

- The human brain can successfully process 6-7 ideas during one time period and maintain good retention of the information *if* enough repetition is used.

- It is less tiring to "spread out" study periods rather than to "cram."

- Pace yourself.

- Be organized.

- Use the tasks/assignments that do not require great amounts of concentration alternately with more difficult tasks.

- Be sure your study activities are in tune with your intentions.

- Begin with the most difficult tasks — and "get it done" so that it won't hang over your head!

- Make studying a habit.

- Build on your learning strengths.

- Seriously consider the effects of procrastination and how well you can do without them.

- Examine your priorities and how you can make changes to make your life easier and more successful.

- Become aware of your time management patterns and change them gradually to better meet your needs.

- Learn to use spare moments: standing in line, waiting for someone or something, etc.

- Make sure you understand the assignment.

- Break large assignments into smaller, organized parts.

- Set reasonable time limits for yourself.

- Give yourself enough time to do a good job. Go for quality!

- Try new ways to solve problems.

- Always predict the amount of effort and the time required to complete a task.

- Don't spread yourself too thin. Consider your commitments and the priority of each.

- Really enjoy your "free time."

- Have a positive attitude about learning.

- It's OK to dislike the assignment or task, but do it anyway!

- Good grades most often are lost due to a lack of organization rather than a lack of information.

- Concentration is the biggest problem when studying.

- Review the information just before you go to bed.

- Prop reading material at a 45 degree angle and your eyes will be less tired.

- Seek help if you don't understand something or if you are having problems.

- Get to know someone in every class you have. You can borrow or trade books, study together, and ask each other questions about assignments.

Steps To Easier Learning

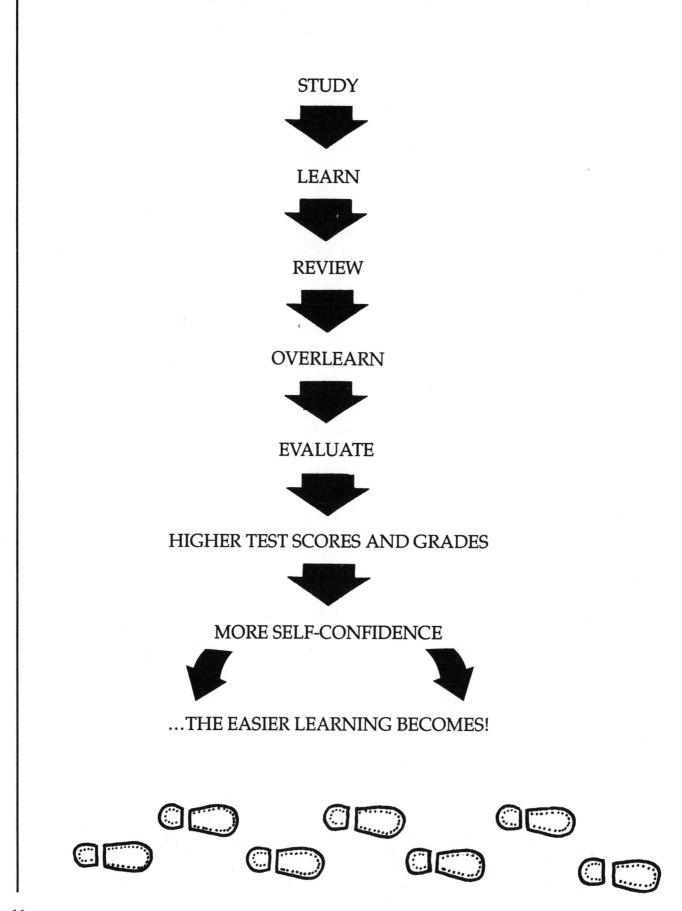

STUDY

LEARN

REVIEW

OVERLEARN

EVALUATE

HIGHER TEST SCORES AND GRADES

MORE SELF-CONFIDENCE

...THE EASIER LEARNING BECOMES!

NOTE-TAKING SKILLS

FOCUS ON
NOTE-TAKING SKILLS

1. Use intentional, focused listening with a positive attitude.

2. Be an active listener and note-taker.

3. Listen 80% and write 20% of the time.

4. Continually add to your personal shorthand system.

5. Review your notes regularly.

6. Match your subject to the right note-taking format.

7. Edit your notes into graphic organizer study sheets.

8. Use color, shapes and placement to your learning advantage.

9. Keep notes together in an organized notebook.

10. Tune out distractions.

OVERVIEW OF NOTE-TAKING SKILLS

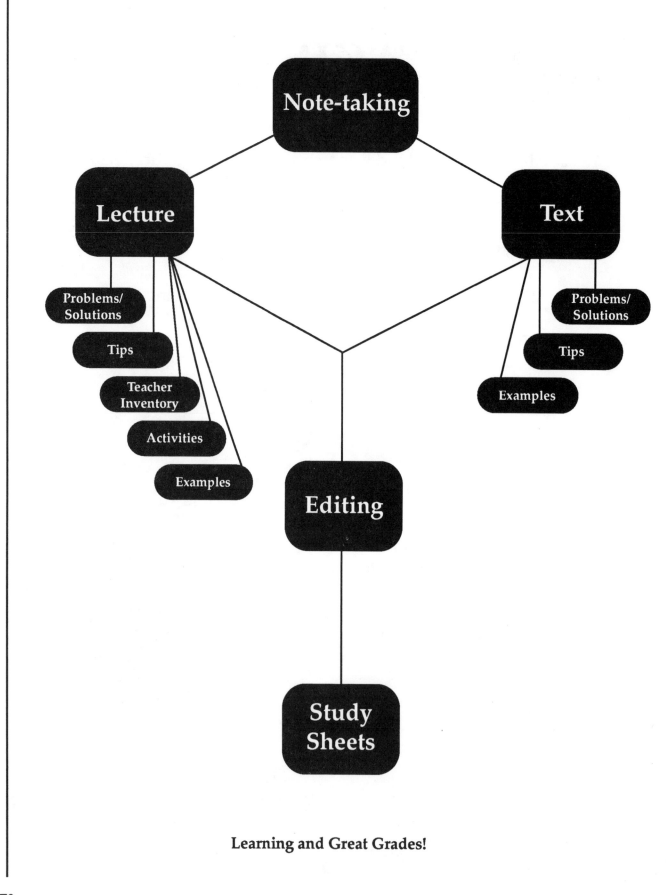

Learning and Great Grades!

Listening and note-taking are two critical classroom survival skills. Without intentional, focused listening, taking accurate notes is impossible. Without effective class notes, learning and retention are greatly reduced.

To be a successful student, good study tools must be correctly and consistently applied with ease. By first evaluating current skills and then integrating new techniques, note-taking can become the tool that ensures success.

Note-taking should be one of your top priorities among all of the study skills. It provides a reference that may be reviewed many times as an aid to memory. Good note-taking methods will make life easier and will help the ongoing process of learning become more meaningful.

ACTIVITIES IN TAKING CLASS NOTES

Evaluate your present note-taking skills by putting a check mark beside each of the note-taking hints that you already practice. Then put a check mark beside those steps that you plan to practice. Leave a space blank if you do not plan to follow a particular strategy.

		Now Do	Plan To Do
1.	Keep a written record of the class.	☐	☐
2.	Sit where the teacher can see me.	☐	☐
3.	Read in advance textbook material about the topic to be presented in class.	☐	☐
4.	Record notes as follows:		
	a. Use 8 1/2" x 11" paper.	☐	☐
	b. Use a sectioned notebook.	☐	☐
	c. Date each day's notes.	☐	☐
	d. Take notes on one side of the page only.	☐	☐
	e. Write legibly.	☐	☐
	f. Abbreviate common words and recurring terms.	☐	☐
	g. Indicate assignments and exams.	☐	☐
5.	Write notes in outline form as follows:		
	a. Start main points at the margin; indent secondary points.	☐	☐
	b. Use white space to show a shift in thought.	☐	☐
6.	Watch for signals of importance:		
	a. Copy whatever the teacher writes on the board.	☐	☐
	b. Write definitions and enumerations.	☐	☐
	c. Write points marked by emphasis words.	☐	☐
	d. Record repeated points.	☐	☐
	e. Note the hints given by the teacher's tone of voice.	☐	☐
7.	Write examples.	☐	☐
8.	Write connecting details and explanations.	☐	☐

From *Senior High Study Skills Booklet*, Jefferson County Schools, Colorado, © 1983. Used by permission.
© 1990 by Incentive Publications, Inc., Nashville, TN.

ACTIVITIES IN TAKING CLASS NOTES *continued*

	Now Do	Plan To Do
9. Do as follows when material is missed:		
a. Leave space for notes missed.	☐	☐
b. Try to get the broad sweep of ideas when falling behind.	☐	☐
10. Question the instructor when an idea isn't clear.	☐	☐
11. Do not stop taking notes during discussion periods.	☐	☐
12. Do not stop taking notes toward the end of class.	☐	☐
13. Go over your notes soon after class.	☐	☐

Now evaluate your skills in studying class notes.

	Now Do	Plan To Do
• Write key words in the margin to recall ideas.	☐	☐
• Turn recall words into questions.	☐	☐
• Use repeated self-testing to learn the material.	☐	☐

From *Senior High Study Skills Booklet*, Jefferson County Schools, Colorado, © 1983. Used by permission.
© 1990 by Incentive Publications, Inc., Nashville, TN.

TERMS FOR TAKING NOTES

Match the following terms with their meanings to check your understanding of key words used to explain note-taking.

Terms

_____ 1. Active Listening

_____ 2. Clarify

_____ 3. Details

_____ 4. Edit

_____ 5. Highlight

_____ 6. Memory Triggers

_____ 7. Main Ideas

_____ 8. Organized Notes

_____ 9. Paraphrasing

_____ 10. Personal Shorthand

_____ 11. Phrases

_____ 12. Raw Notes

_____ 13. Subject Matter

Meaning

A. Arrange material according to topic by subject matter, main idea and detail.

B. To make clear and fully understandable.

C. Cue words and phrases placed in the left-hand column to jog memory.

D. Think about what is said, picking up on all available cues and making some type of response.

E. Material as taken directly from a lecture to be rewritten at a later time.

F. Main divisions: definitions, kind, results, methods. The topic, area or precise division of the subject.

G. To organize, categorize and classify; to add or subtract ideas.

H. Explicit examples, illustrations or statistics.

I. Thought units, <u>not</u> sentences.

J. To focus attention on certain points by underlining or color-coding.

K. Generalization. Subject headings and topics. Central thought; essential point.

L. To express in your own words.

M. Shortened forms or symbols that are meaningful to the note-taker.

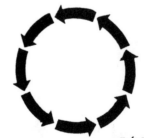

Answers: (1.) D, (2.) B, (3.) H, (4.) G, (5.) J, (6.) C, (7.) K, (8.) A, (9.) L, (10.) M, (11.) I, (12.) E, (13.) F

APPRECIATION
enjoyment
pleasure
records
television

INFORMATION
Instructions
details
lecture
new job

UNDERSTANDING
process information
relate to own
    experience
class discussion

WHY WE DON'T LISTEN

A. Input Overload
1. One third of our "awake time" is spent listening.
2. Attention wanders at times.

B. Brain Power
1. The brain is capable of understanding speech at 600 words per minute.
2. The average person speaks 100 to 140 words per minute.
3. What does your mind do with all of the "leftover" time?

C. Physical Noise
1. Sounds in the environment interfere.
2. Physical surroundings are uncomfortable.
3. Fatigue distracts.

D. Personal Concerns
1. Emotional problems and/or thoughts occupy the mind and block out auditory input.

E. Talking Seems More Important

F. Listening Skills Not Taught
1. Listening skills not continually/consistently practiced.

G. "Tune In" Too Late
1. Individuals do not listen from the start of the lecture/conversation.

H. Not Listening Ahead
1. Individuals do not process and remember/associate what is being said now.

1. "Set" your mind — intend to listen.

2. Listen to *what* is being said — don't allow your mind to wander.

3. Clarify continually (to yourself) what is being said.

4. Keep your mind active — take notes.

5. Resist distractions (physical, emotional, mental).

6. Involve yourself — think of examples as the speaker talks.

7. Listen very closely to introductory and concluding remarks/ideas.

8. Anticipate what is coming next (this is the most difficult yet the most effective for your memory).

9. Pay attention to "speaker cues" (voice, physical motions, rate of speech).

10. Think of questions while listening (helps to organize thoughts).

11. Constantly try to link concepts and main ideas with details as well as cause/effect and problem-solving techniques.

12. Listen for what is *not* said as well as what *is* said.

13. Listen to class discussions carefully and make note of any points the speaker reinforces.

14. Note any material that is repeated.

15. Always summarize the information.

PERSONAL SHORTHAND METHOD

Each individual should develop a "personal shorthand method" to become more efficient and effective in note-taking skills. This will allow the individual to put more information on the paper with less effort and stress.

This method should be personalized by the individual in order to fully gain the most benefit from the process and product. This also allows for a more consistent and natural system for years to come.

 Look over your notes from a recent class to see how many times you repeat the same words. Make a list of these words.

 Decide upon a symbol or abbreviation for each word so that you can write these words faster. Make a list of the words and their abbreviations/symbols and put it in your notebook. Keep your notebook in a convenient place so that you may refer to the list often while you take notes until you become very familiar and comfortable with the system you have developed.

Here are a few examples that you can use:

b/c	=	because		w/o	=	without
.'.	=	therefore		govt	=	government
w/	=	with		b/f	=	before
--->	=	to follow		rt	=	right
cont.	=	continue		*	=	important
+	=	and		intro	=	introduction

Step 3

When you are taking notes from a "specialized lecture" in which a specific topic will be covered (requiring a special, repeated vocabulary), you will need to create a code just for this onetime purpose. Make a box in the upper left corner of a piece of paper and write the symbols and their meanings for this specific purpose in the box. Be sure to leave space for additions as you may need to add some as the lecture progresses. You always can refer to this box during the lecture and when you review/edit your notes.

PERSONAL SHORTHAND METHOD *continued*

Here is an example of the box created on the note-taking paper for the specialized abbreviations/symbols:

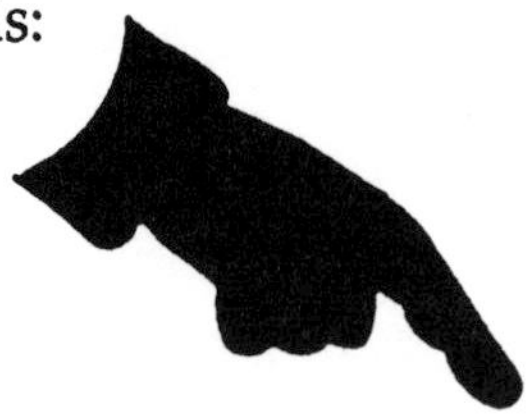

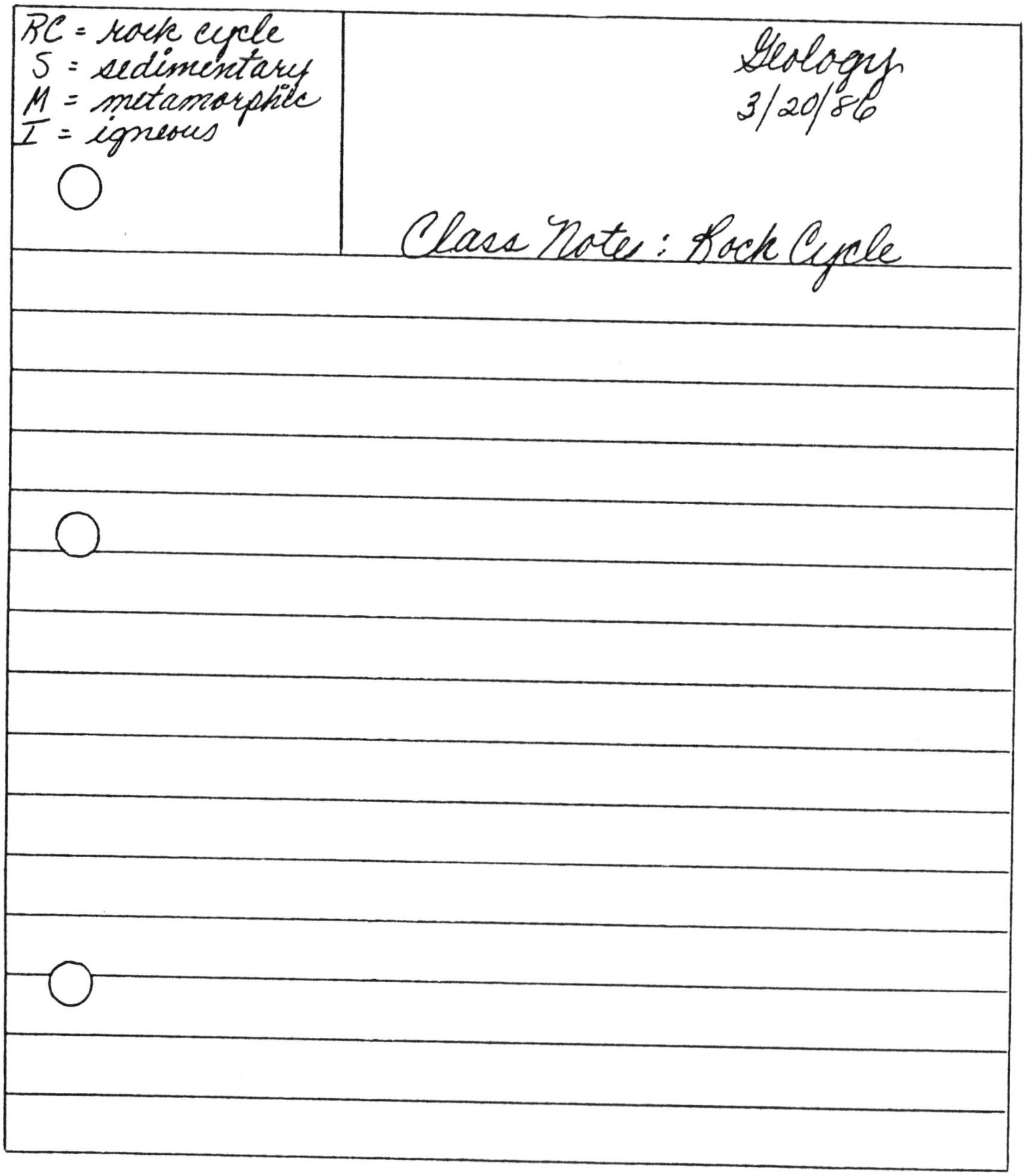

RC = rock cycle
S = sedimentary
M = metamorphic
I = igneous
Geology
3/20/86
Class Notes: Rock Cycle

- Within two weeks you forget 80% of what you hear!

- Within four weeks you remember only 5% of what you hear!

WHY TAKE NOTES?

Because our memories fade quickly and teachers expect us to remember and apply facts we learn, writing information so that it can be used at a later time is probably the most valuable study aid. Learning to take effective and efficient notes helps you to be an active learner and involves you in the process of learning. Organized note-taking from lectures will lead to longer memory and better grades!

I. BEFORE CLASS

A. Skim or review any text/material assigned or notes from previous classes.

B. Gather all materials needed:
1. Notebook/paper
2. Text
3. Several pens (not pencils)
4. Any handouts necessary

C. Intend to be an active listener and note-taker.

D. Plan to arrive in class with enough time to get organized.
1. Make sure your "equipment" is in place.
2. Open your text to the proper place.
3. Set your mind on listening and writing.
   a. Listen 80% of the time.
   b. Write 20% of the time.

E. **Sit in the front of the room.**
1. Avoid distractions from those sitting in front of you.
2. Sit in the teacher's line of vision to stay "in tune" and focused.

F. **Date and head your paper before class begins to save time.**

II. HINTS FOR TAKING EFFECTIVE/EFFICIENT CLASSROOM NOTES

A. **Use an 8 1/2" x 11" notebook or three-ring binder with paper of the same size.**
1. Leave spaces between the lines so that notes may be added later.
2. Draw margins before class and use them when taking notes.
3. Leave space at the top of the paper for personal shorthand codes.

B. **Write legibly.**

C. **Develop and consistently use a personal shorthand method.**

D. **Choose one system that suits the information to be presented and stay with it.**

E. **Write assignment/test dates in the same place all the time.**

F. **Stay focused — don't pay too much attention to others.**

III. DURING CLASS

A. **Write main ideas.**
1. Write the points your teacher emphasizes and repeats.
2. Major ideas are the main ideas which are supported by:
    a. Details
    b. Explanations
    c. General discussions
    d. Examples
    e. Inclusion in the introductory and closing comments

B. Write important details.
1. Include all supporting information for main ideas.
2. Record details that connect and explain main points.

C. Watch for signals of importance.
1. Copy whatever the teacher writes on the chalkboard.
2. Always write definitions and listings:
   a. "The four steps in this process…"
   b. "Seven characteristics are…"
   c. "The two causes are…"
   d. "These four reasons are…"
3. Listen for important remarks such as:
   a. "And don't forget…"
   b. "This is an important reason…"
   c. "Pay special attention to…"
   d. "The basic idea is…"
   e. "…and I'll keep coming back to the idea that…"
4. Note the teacher's physical gestures.
   a. Pointing
   b. Listing with fingers
   c. Facial expressions
   d. Stepping forward
   e. Pounding on desk, etc.

5. Listen to the teacher's voice and note:
   a. Change in speed
   b. Change in volume
   c. Change of pitch

D. Make special notes of repeated information in the left margin.

E. **Don't hesitate to raise your hand and ask a question.**
   1. Many others probably are in need of the same information.
   2. Teachers look favorably upon students who show interest and curiosity.

F. **Don't stop taking notes during discussion periods or toward the end of class.**
   1. Teachers often give the most important ideas during the last five minutes of class.

IV. **AFTER CLASS**

A. **Ask the teacher questions if appropriate.**

B. **Ask another student to help you fill in any notes you didn't get during class.**

C. **Briefly review your notes within 24 hours.**

D. **Edit your notes within 24 hours.**

I. BE AN EFFECTIVE TEXT NOTE-TAKER

A. Get the right amount of information:
1. Too much = too long to reread and remember.
2. Too little = no meaning between main ideas and supporting details.

B. Notes must be consistent and organized.
1. Develop a system and use it — don't be afraid to make changes for improvement.
2. Code your notes in the left margin.
    a. Use checks for main ideas.
    b. Use stars for details, points, etc.

C. Strive to be very accurate.

D. Your notes should show the content of the text.
1. Be sure to get the author's meaning and not just your ideas.
2. Note new vocabulary words and their meanings.

II. ONE METHOD

A. Briefly preview the entire reading selection.
1. Skim or scan the first to last pages and look for:
    a. Main headings and subheadings and relationships between the two
    b. Pictures, graphs, charts
    c. Questions at the "end" or summaries
    d. Organization and format of the particular selection
2. Review if necessary.

B. **Based on the organization of the material, determine the best *matching* organization for your notes.**
1. Outline (formal or informal)
2. Graphic organizer or mind maps
3. The Cornell Method
4. Sequencing
5. Laddering
6. Chart

C. **Divide the information into blocks according to topics.**

D. **Read through an entire block first, then go back and take notes on the main ideas and supporting details.**

E. **Take a ten-minute break after each 30 - 45 minute concentrated study period.**

F. **After completing the last block of notes:**
1. Take five minutes to reread your notes.
2. Be sure you understand the main ideas and their relationships to each other — be sure all words in italics are included.
3. Reread the introduction or conclusion to see if all of the main points mentioned are covered in your notes.
4. Use the items mentioned in number III, "Uses for left margin," to quiz yourself.

III. USES FOR LEFT MARGIN

A. Mark one to two inches on the left side of the paper and use the space for the following:

1. Summary words/short phrases to "jog" the memory
2. Cue words for further action you need to take:
   a. Reread
   b. Test item
   c. Ask question
   d. Summarize
3. Color -coding system:
   a. Words and definitions
   b. Lists/numbered items
   c. Causes/effects
4. Possible symbols:

ex - example	$\widehat{T}$ - good test question
R^2 - reread	? - confusing; need explanation
S - summary	* - important
D - definition	Make up more of your own!

? **What is it?**

- A system of correcting, revising and adding to your text or lecture notes

? **Why edit?**

- To make your notes more accurate and complete
- To organize your notes

& **How to edit:**

- Read your notes.
- Plan to spend 5 to 10 minutes per one set of notes.
- Try to edit within 24 hours after taking the notes.
- Color-code:
    - main ideas
    - details
    - definitions
    - words in italics
    - information stressed by the teacher
        - Turn headings into questions and try to answer them.
        - Replace the shorthand system with complete thoughts where needed.
        - Clarify points and meanings and make connections.
        - Add personal insights.
        - List questions to ask the teacher.
        - Use a recall clue system:
            - Leave a 1" - 2" left margin.
            - When editing notes, add words to trigger your memory.
            - Cover the right side of the paper and use the words in the column to test yourself as you edit.

WHAT ARE STUDY SHEETS?

Study sheets are very complete notes that you can use to study. They are a combination of lecture and text notes as well as research information and your own ideas.

WHY MAKE AND USE STUDY SHEETS?

By combining all of your notes and information, it forces you to concentrate on your notes while you rewrite the main ideas and important details one more time. The notes are reduced into an efficient and effective format for studying. Since everything is now in one place, you can put away the books and the many pages of notes.

STEPS IN CONSTRUCTING STUDY SHEETS:

1. Review all notes and information.
2. Organize the notes by topics:
   - Spread out the notes on a table or floor so that you can see them.
   - Use paper clips to hold them together.
3. Combine all important information, using one sheet per topic.
   - Sift through the important main ideas and supporting details.
   - Write on only one side of the paper (this allows you to spread them out so that you can see all of them at once).
4. Leave a margin on the left side in which to write recall clues.
   - Recall clues are words or simple phrases that jog your memory and signal important information.
   - Use the margin to note sources (books, pages, dates).
5. Make an overview sheet for each chapter or block of material.
   - Use outlines, graphic organizers and mind maps.
   - This gives a quick, comprehensive view.
   - It brings main ideas and details together.
   - It makes things easier to remember.

continued

6. Write legibly so that you can concentrate on studying your notes (not duplicating them).
   - Always use a pen (pencils smear).
7. Use color-coded highlighters or pens.
   - Separate main ideas and details.
   - Highlight vocabulary words and definitions.
8. Write words and short phrases.
   - They're easier for the mind to remember.
   - They're less bulky.
9. Decide on *one* organizational system and use it throughout the study sheets.
10. Use 3" x 5" cards.
    - Write one idea on a card.

IF YOU CONSTRUCTED THOROUGH AND COMPREHENSIVE STUDY SHEETS...

- you no longer need lecture notes, text notes, etc.
- your organization will give you better use of study time and "brain power"
- you will know that you have done a good job, and this will reduce test anxiety
- give yourself a reward!

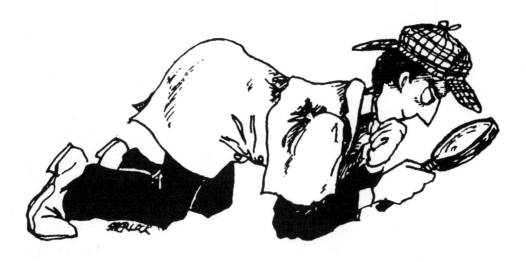

#1

Recall Column	Main Ideas & Details	Your Ideas
words phrases sources	Combine all notes in an organized system here. Outline, indent, or use some other system.	

#2

Recall Column	Textbook Notes	Lecture/Class Notes
words phrases sources	Take notes here as you read the textbook, or condense text notes for a study sheet.	Condense class notes here (parallel to text notes).

TIPS FOR MAKING NOTE-TAKING EASIER

- Have a positive attitude — intend to learn when taking notes!

- Keep notes in a notebook and keep notebooks together in a folder or carrying case.

- Use only ink (erasable pens are great) — pencils smear and fade.

- Use a separate notebook for each class — leave room for an assignment calendar.

- Use standard size notebooks and paper.

- Save time by staying organized!

- Write on only one side of the paper.

- Leave a 1" - 2" left margin — mark the margins ahead of time, before you need the paper.

- Leave "heading room" for a box to contain special codes.

- Always write the topic and date at the top of the page.

- Underline any emphasized information on handouts.

- Circle unclear information.

- Leave blank spaces between lines so that you can add information later.

- Don't try to write every word or thought.

- Sit in the front of the class to avoid distractions and to see better!

- Listen more than you write.

- Take notes from class discussions, student comments, diagrams, charts, overhead transparencies, and the last five minutes of class!

- Listen closely to lecture introductions and summaries.

- Pay attention to concluding statements of films.

- BE ORGANIZED!

PROBLEMS IN NOTE-TAKING • AND HOW TO SOLVE THEM

Lecture:

Speaker	Notes
1. Well-organized	1. Notes are easy to take and will be well-organized.
2. Talks too fast; speaks in a monotone or has a speech problem.	2. Try to adjust your ears and mind quickly; be a good listener.
3. The speaker is boring.	3. Force yourself to become an "active listener." Guess what's coming next, make connecting points with the material presented, and think of questions to ask.
4. Uses difficult vocabulary	4. Read the text the speaker will cover before the lecture. Wait until after the lecture to look up difficult words.
5. Leafs through the text while speaking.	5. Be sure to have your text close at hand. Identify or note important paragraphs.
6. The speaker rambles.	6. Write something about each topic mentioned. Listen for introductory and concluding statements.
7. Digresses to relate personal experiences and examples	7. Rest your mind, but be alert to any important main ideas or details.
8. You do not like the speaker.	8. Don't waste time or energy thinking about why you do not like the speaker. You need the information, so get on with note-taking!

PROBLEMS IN NOTE-TAKING • AND HOW TO SOLVE THEM

continued

Reading/Text:

Problem	Solution
1. The text is boring.	1. Break the information into small units. Read an entire unit and then go back and take notes. Set a goal of completing so many units and then reward yourself!
2. Your mind wanders.	2. Make a check or "tic" on a separate sheet of paper each time you realize that your mind is wandering. Set a goal to make fewer tic marks for each assignment.
3. The vocabulary is difficult.	3. Try to read through the information without stopping. Use context clues as much as possible. After reading, look up difficult words and write the definitions.
4. There's too much material and not enough time.	4. Form a study group. Divide the material to be covered and assign specific pages, chapters, etc., to each member. Ask each member to take thorough notes and study the information. Then return to the group and orally share the assigned material. Give photocopies of all notes to every group member.
5. You still don't understand the material after reading it numerous times.	5. Form a study group (see above) and talk it through with friends. Seek tutors in your school or community.

Teacher Inventory

Teacher's Name	Verbal/Nonverbal Clues	Materials Most Often Used	Hints, Systems, Methods I Will Use

SAMPLE FORMS FOR NOTE-TAKING

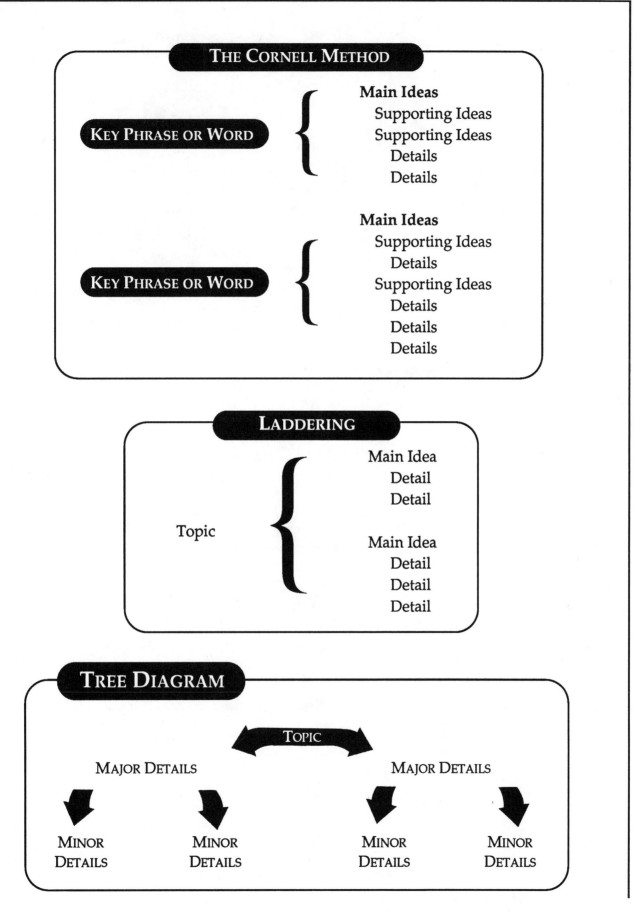

THE CORNELL METHOD

KEY PHRASE OR WORD {
Main Ideas
Supporting Ideas
Supporting Ideas
Details
Details

KEY PHRASE OR WORD {
Main Ideas
Supporting Ideas
Details
Supporting Ideas
Details
Details
Details

LADDERING

Topic {
Main Idea
Detail
Detail

Main Idea
Detail
Detail
Detail

TREE DIAGRAM

TOPIC

MAJOR DETAILS   MAJOR DETAILS

MINOR   MINOR   MINOR   MINOR
DETAILS   DETAILS   DETAILS   DETAILS

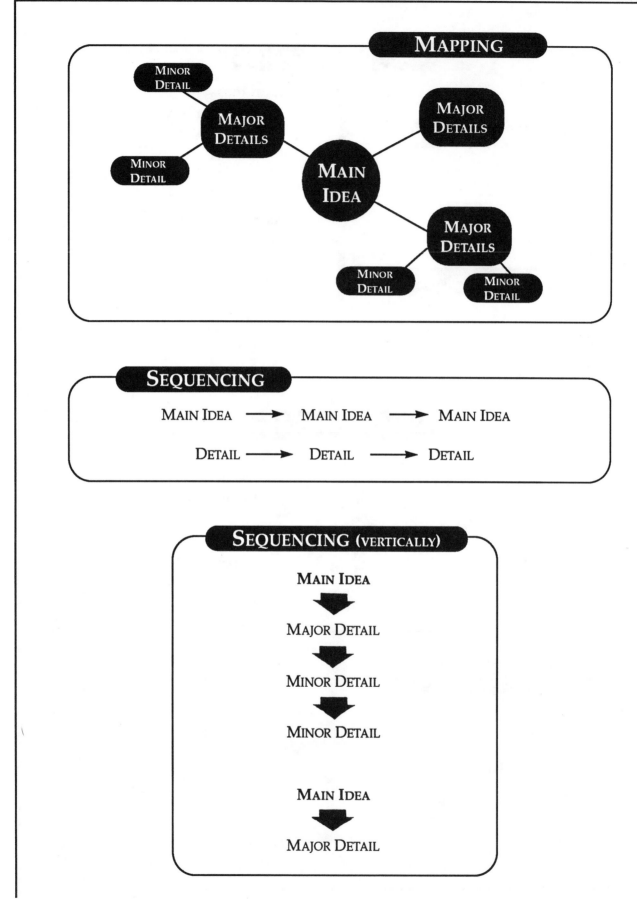

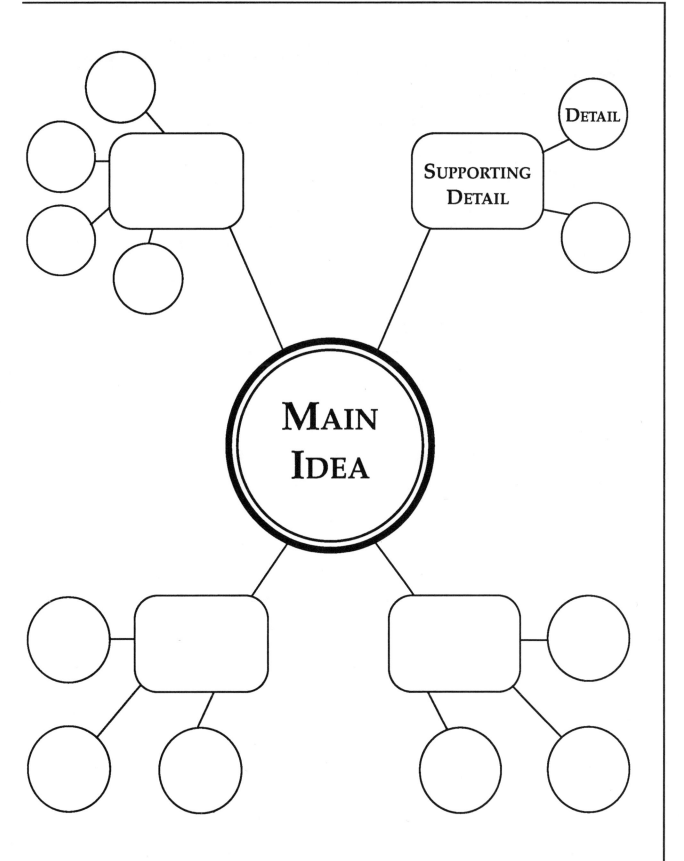

GRAPHIC ORGANIZER

MAIN IDEAS　　　　　**SUPPORTING IDEAS**　　　　　**DETAILS**

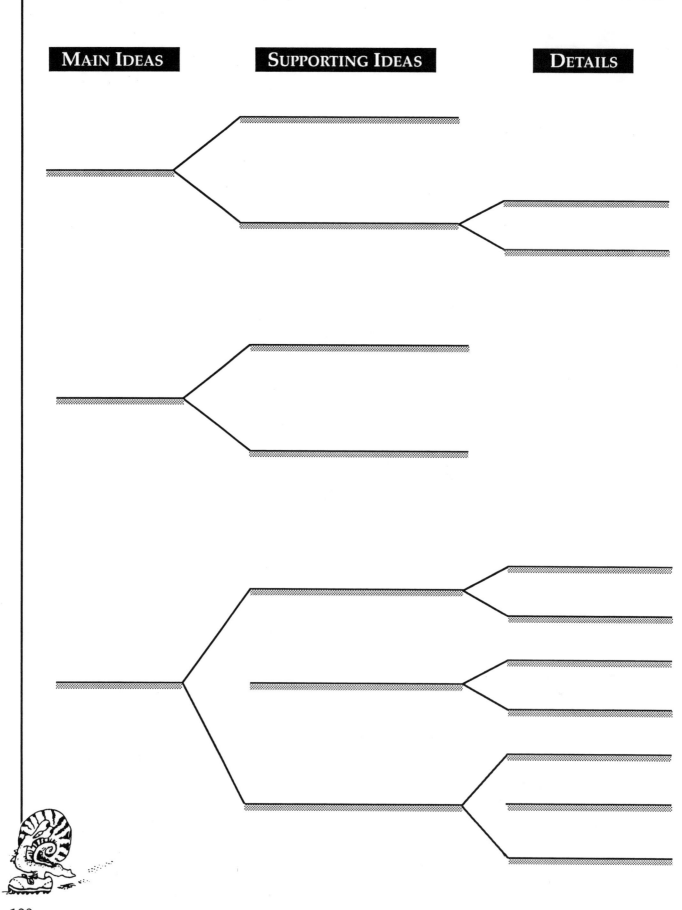

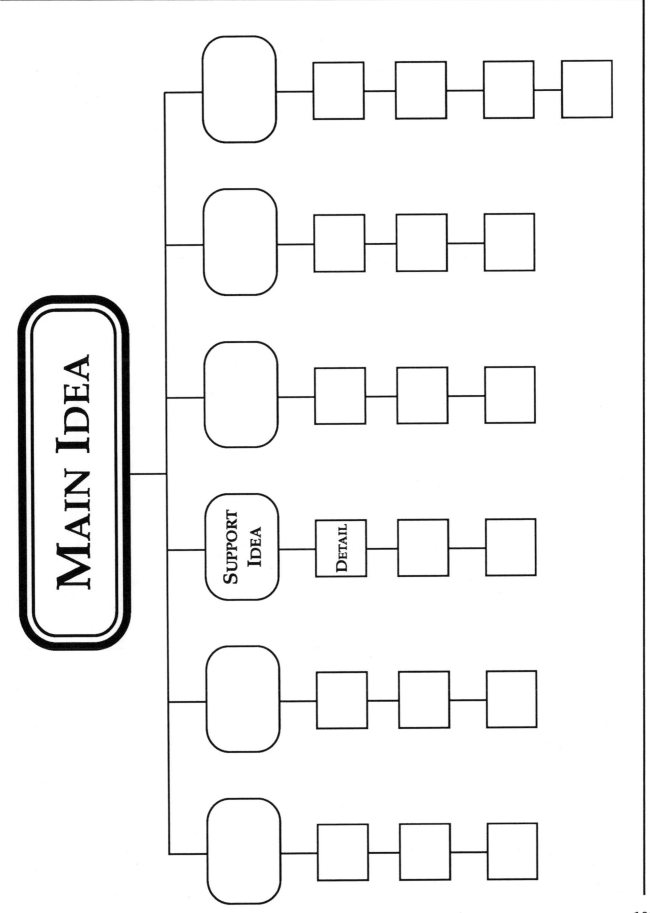

MAIN IDEA

SUPPORT IDEA

DETAIL

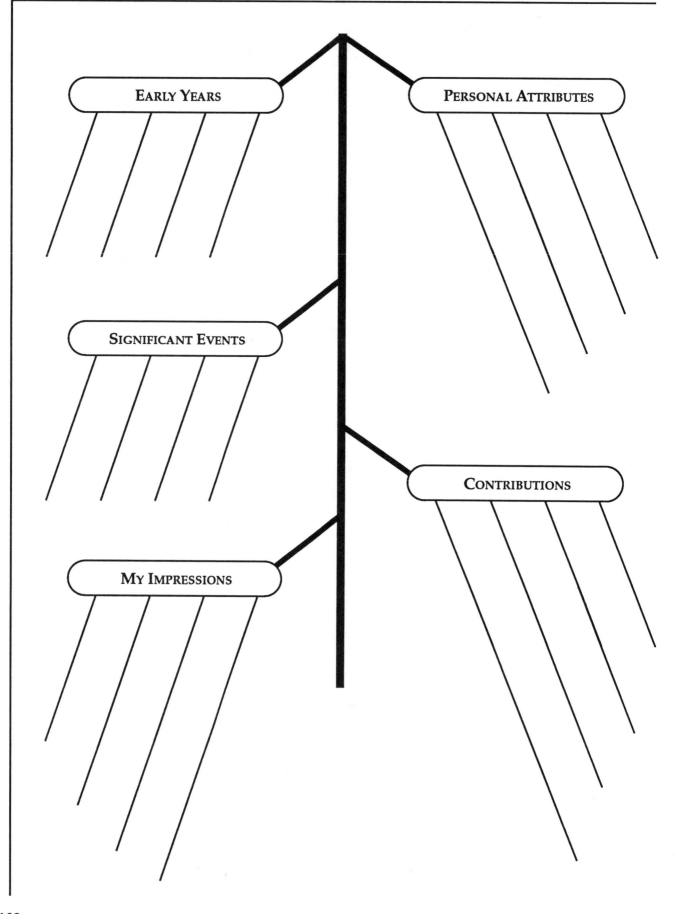

EARLY YEARS

PERSONAL ATTRIBUTES

SIGNIFICANT EVENTS

CONTRIBUTIONS

MY IMPRESSIONS

GRAPHIC ORGANIZER • "TREE OUTLINE"

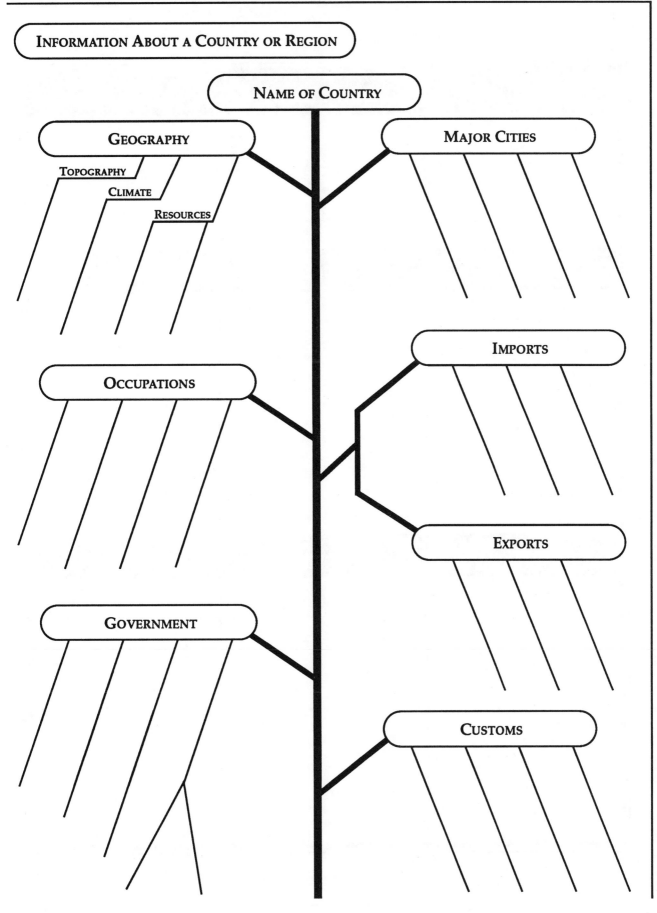

INFORMATION ABOUT A COUNTRY OR REGION

NAME OF COUNTRY

GEOGRAPHY

MAJOR CITIES

TOPOGRAPHY

CLIMATE

RESOURCES

OCCUPATIONS

IMPORTS

EXPORTS

GOVERNMENT

CUSTOMS

NOTE-TAKING ORGANIZER

MAIN IDEA	MAIN IDEA	MAIN IDEA

SUPPORTING	SUPPORTING	SUPPORTING
1.	1.	1.
2.	2.	2.
3.	3.	3.
4.	4.	4.
5.	5.	5.
6.	6.	6.
7.	7.	7.

DETAILS	DETAILS	DETAILS
1.	1.	1.
2.	2.	2.
3.	3.	3.
4.		4.
5.		5.
6.		6.
7.		7.
		8.

I.

    A.

    B.

    C.

        1.

        2.

        3.

II.   A.

    B.

        1.

        2.

            a.

            b.

            c.

III.   A.

        1.

        2.

        3.

            a.

            b.

                1.

                2.

                    a.

                    b.

                    c.

    B.

STUDENT STUDY GUIDE

1. Read through the material.
2. Complete the chart.
3. Cover each side one at a time and quiz yourself.

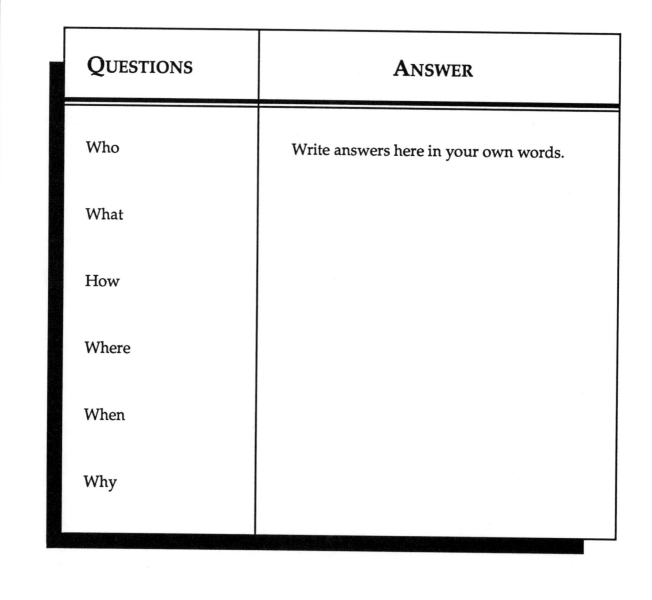

QUESTIONS	ANSWER
Who	Write answers here in your own words.
What	
How	
Where	
When	
Why	

Write one concept or idea on each card.

KEY WORDS   CODE

(Keyed to book,
study sheet, etc.)

One concept here.

Supporting details here.

THE DIVIDED PAGE

LITERATURE NOTE-MAKING METHOD

3" x 5" or 5" x 7" note cards

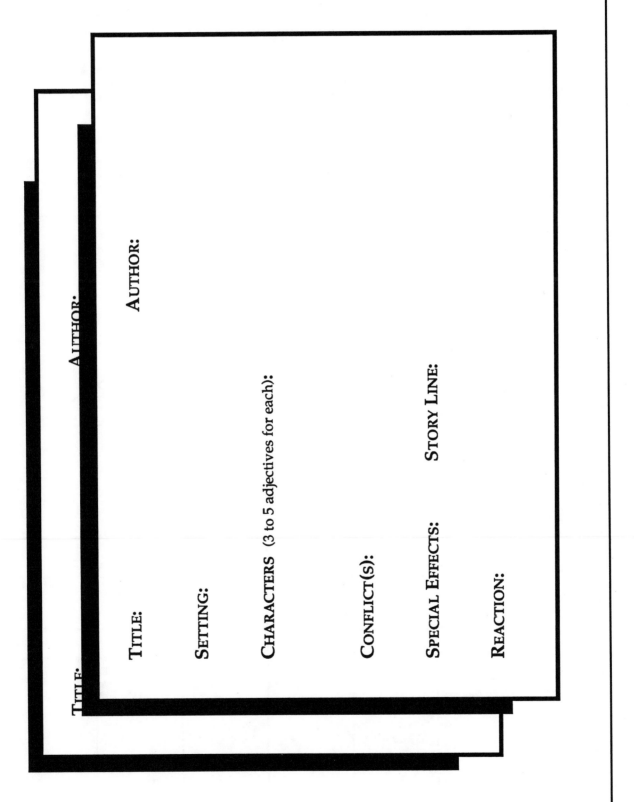

AUTHOR:

AUTHOR:

TITLE:

TITLE:

SETTING:

CHARACTERS (3 to 5 adjectives for each):

CONFLICT(S):

SPECIAL EFFECTS:

STORY LINE:

REACTION:

ENUMERATIVE

Topic Sentence:

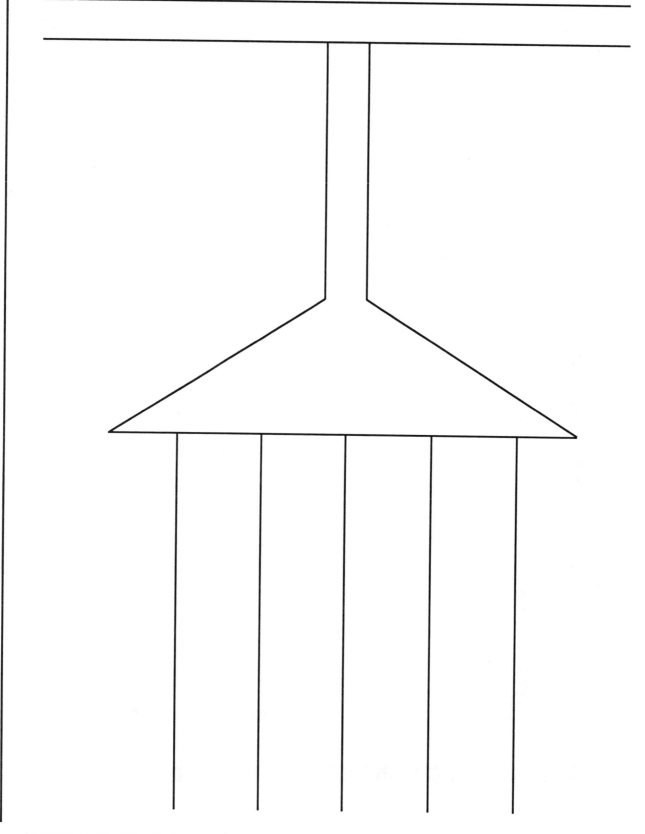

SEQUENCE

GENERAL TOPIC: _____

1. _____
SPECIFIC TOPIC   (List detail below)

SPECIFIC TOPIC _____

SPECIFIC TOPIC _____

CAUSE/EFFECT

TOPIC SENTENCE:

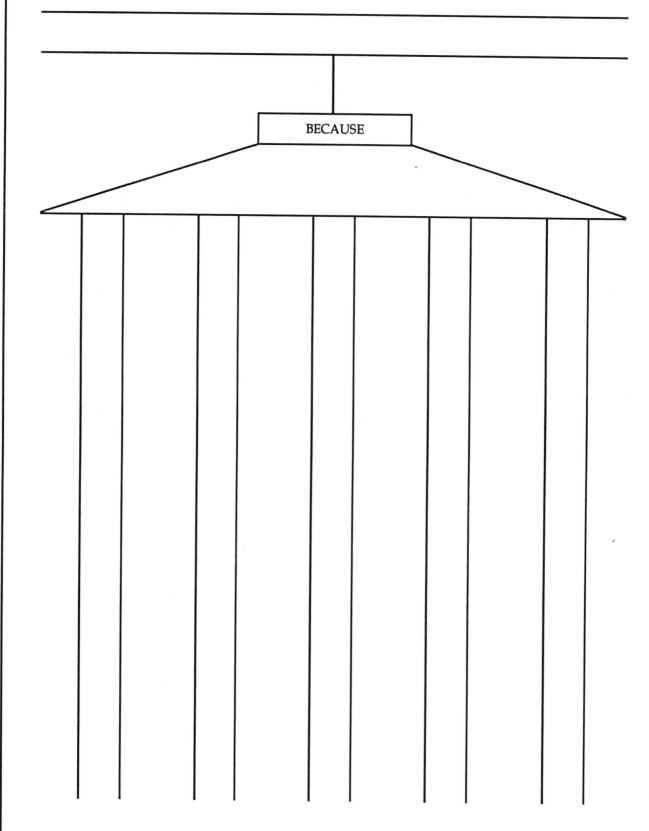

BECAUSE

COMPARISON/CONTRAST

TOPIC SENTENCE:

SUBJECTS

SIMILARITIES

DIFFERENCES

DESCRIPTION

TOPIC SENTENCE:

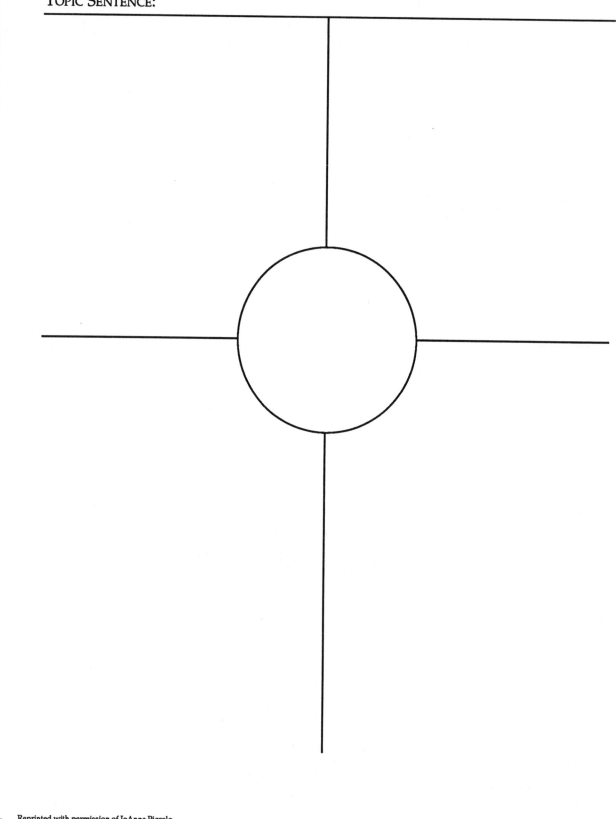

READING SKILLS

Focus On Reading Skills

1. Determine reading purpose and rate before beginning.

2. Intend to remember what you read.

3. Use SQ3R.

4. Know your textbook and how to use it.

5. Learn to predict, clarify and summarize.

6. Question while you read – read to answer the questions.

7. Read then recite what you read.

8. Discuss what you read.

9. Review what you already know about the topic before reading.

10. Watch for "signal words" that indicate main ideas and important details.

READING

Reading is a primary source for gaining information and learning. Just as there are any number of ways and reasons to do anything, so it is with reading. To learn, apply and master specific reading strategies is to make study time more efficient and effective. It is time well-spent. In fact, it is guaranteed to save you time in the long run.

There are numerous aids that you can use to increase your reading "brain power." Prereading techniques give you an "overview" and help you determine the importance of the materials as well as your purpose and rate for reading. Flexible reading habits lead to quality study skills and increased memory. Learning how to survey textbooks, spot "signal words," skim, find main ideas, check for comprehension, and read illustrations definitely will improve your understanding and grades. So, give the following reading hints, tips and methods a try, and soon they will become habits you won't want to break!

There are many ways to do any one thing — many approaches to solving a problem, painting a picture, and achieving desired results. Reading for different purposes is no different. You probably would not read a newspaper in the same manner and with the same goal as you would read a science textbook. You would read a pamphlet about how to construct a bookshelf differently than a novel or short story.

It is very important that the purpose and kind of material be appropriate for your reading speed. First, determine the type of material you are going to read. Find out if it is:

- review material/information
- new information
- fiction
- nonfiction
- technical
- purely for enjoyment

Secondly, set your purpose for reading the selection by asking yourself:

- "Why am I reading this?"
    ...for a test
    ...for enjoyment
    ...for the main ideas
    ...to discuss later
    ...to get an overall, general view

- "What is my end goal?"
    mastery
    understanding the concept
    understanding the plot/characters

- "What am I expected to remember?"
    details
    author's mood, opinion, intent
    sequence of events
    cause/effect
    relationships

Once you clearly understand your goal and the type of reading material, match these with an appropriate reading rate (see page 121).

IN SUMMARY...

1. Determine type of material
2. Set purpose
3. Decide reading rate
4. Read

FIVE DIFFERENT READING RATES

STRATEGY FOR RATE OF READING	PURPOSE	MATERIALS
1. Scanning	1. Gives a sense of main topics and ideas; gives clear picture of overall organization. Use to find a specific detail such as a date, name, country, answer to question, etc. *Do not read all of the words.*	1. dictionary; listings/lists; newspapers; magazine articles
2. Skimming	2. To find main ideas, cause/effect; to survey for general ideas. To recognize sequences & relationships between headings/subheadings. To identify the topic. To look for italicized words/phrases. Use as "pre-reading" of more difficult materials. *Do not read all of the words.*	2. easy-to-read print; magazines; fiction; previewing texts
3. Rapid Reading	3. To read all of the words at a fast rate. To search for specific information.	3. same as #2 – but read for main ideas and their details
4. Slow Reading	4. To find all of the available information. *Take notes and/or underline.*	4. any textbook to be read for details; technical articles
5. Careful Reading	5. To find procedures; to follow step-by-step instructions; to analyze and evaluate content. *Take detailed notes or outline.*	5. complex ideas or concepts; non-fiction, sequential/detailed reports; poetry, scientific data or texts

HOW TO SKIM

 PURPOSE

As quickly as possible, selectively read the material to find specific information and to survey for general ideas.

 WHEN

You are *not* responsible for details or in-depth comprehension.
You want/need a prereading exercise to familiarize yourself with the material.

WHY

To avoid reading what you don't need to read.
To save time.
To get an overall view…in a hurry.
To determine if you need to read further.

HOW

Do not read every word, just…

1. Read main titles.
2. Read subtitles — look for specific names, dates, lists, etc., in each paragraph.
3. Glance at any illustrations, pictures, charts, etc.
4. Read first and last sentences of each paragraph if time permits.
5. Read the questions at the end of the paragraph/chapter.

Always know *why* you are skimming the material and for *what* specific things you are looking.

HOW TO FIND THE MAIN IDEA

Main ideas help you to recognize and remember supporting details. They are the "topics" of entire paragraphs or selections. Main ideas often are found in first or last sentences/paragraphs, but they can be located anywhere within the material.

When trying to find the main idea:
- Determine what the topic of the paragraph is. "What is being discussed?"
- Determine what it says about the concept. "What is the author saying?"
- Make up a statement that would include all of the details.
- Check to see if the statement (main idea) covers only the information in that particular paragraph.

You also can find the main ideas in paragraphs by looking for the strategies authors choose to use in delivering their information, ideas or concepts. They are:

first or last sentence	important ideas stated in the opening or closing statements
examples	lists of specific traits, actions and ideas that illustrate the main idea
comparison/contrast	relating how something is alike or different from something else
vocabulary	notice descriptive words and what one or two concepts they describe; look for italics and boldface type

analogies   comparisons of the relationships of ideas, concepts or things

figurative speech   the use of one word or phrase to describe

reading between the lines   what is not there but is implied

enumeration   listing of ideas

transition   shows a change from one idea to another

descriptive   demonstrates how something looks, sounds or feels

methodological   tells how you do something; gives step-by-step directions

introductory   may begin with questions and give definitions; signals the reader what the chapter is about

summary   sometimes begins with "In summary" or "In conclusion"; usually the last paragraph

definition   used to qualify, describe, characterize, compare or contrast, give the limits of or tell by anecdote

Signal words tell you what's coming and what to watch for as well as what you already have read. They may signal a list, summary, comparison/contrast, detail, main idea, beginning or ending.

Watching for signal words as you skim or scan will immediately focus your attention or "signal" you to make note of the information to follow.

Listed below and on the next page are some signal words and their "meanings":

READ ON —MORE IS COMING
and   *first*
more   *second*
moreover   *third*
furthermore   *also*
besides   *finally*
some   *primarily*
many   *a key feature*
for one thing   *in addition*
likewise   *next*
main
another

CONCLUSION/SUMMARY
therefore
thus
finally
in conclusion
consequently
hence
as a result
in summary
noteworthy
last of all

WORDS THAT ILLUSTRATE
for example
to illustrate
specifically
for instance
such as
following are

REVERSE YOUR THINKING

yet
however
but
otherwise
nevertheless
still
in spite of
likewise
in contrast
instead
even though

WORDS OF IMPORTANCE

better	*best*
most	*good*
least	*important*
most of all	*chief factor*
above all	*less*
worst	*bad*
major	*minor*
all	*some*
few	

CAUSE/EFFECT WORDS

it is because
because
unless
as a result
effect
cause
the quality
attribute
for this reason
if
consequently

WORDS THAT DEFINE

referred to as
is
the same as
means
termed
defined as
means the same
a synonym for

COMPARISON/CONTRAST WORDS

more	*than*
compares	*nevertheless*
otherwise	*contrasts*
differences	*likeness*
similar	*similarly*
alike	

Each time you receive a textbook that is new to you, take time to become acquainted with the parts of the book and how the teacher views the textbook. Following are some questions which you may want to ask yourself as you look through the book.

AUTHOR OR AUTHORS

- Who wrote the book?
- What information is given about the author or authors?
- Did the author or authors write a section for the student?
- Does the book have a preface that explains how the book came to be written and how the book might be used?

ORGANIZATION

- How is the book organized?
- What does the table of contents tell about the organization of the book?
- Is the organization historical, chronological, factual or other?
- Does the book have chapters and/or units?

TIMELINESS

- When was the book written?
- Will the age of the book and its information be a problem in this class?
- Will you need to refer to other sources for more recent information?

From *Senior High Study Skills Booklet*, Jefferson County Schools, © 1983. Used by permission.
© 1990 by Incentive Publications, Inc., Nashville, TN.

BOOK PARTS

- Does the book have an index?
- Does the book have a glossary?
- Does the book have a bibliography?
- Does the book have an appendix or appendices?

MORE ORGANIZATIONAL POINTS

- How are the various sections, units and/or chapters organized?
- How is new vocabulary handled?
- Are new topics introduced in boldface type?
- Does the author include study questions?
- Does each section/chapter have an introduction and a summary?

NOTES AND OUTLINING

- What kind of notes will I need to take while reading the text?
- Can the sections be easily outlined?
- At what rate will I read and study this textbook?

GRAPHIC AIDS

- How are the illustrations handled in the book?
- Are graphic aids included such as graphs, charts, tables?

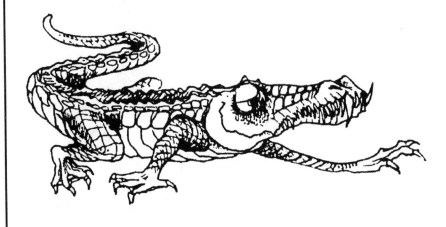

From *Senior High Study Skills Booklet*, Jefferson County Schools, © 1983. Used by permission.
© 1990 by Incentive Publications, Inc., Nashville, TN.

PREVIEWING A TEXTBOOK ASSIGNMENT

Previewing a textbook is important and can save you time in the long run. It gives you a much better overall picture and forces you to set your mind on the topic so that you can "zero in" on the main ideas. Follow these brief and simple steps for your next textbook reading assignment.

 STUDY THE TITLE
- This gives the shortest possible summary of the entire selection.
- What do you already know about the topic, or about what do you think the topic will be concerned?

 QUICKLY READ OVER FIRST AND LAST PARAGRAPHS
- This gives the main ideas.
- "See" relationships between the main ideas.

READ HEADINGS/SUBHEADINGS
- "See" relationships between them.
- These relationships often are the keys to important ideas.
- Main Headings: larger type, capital letters, colored/darker ink
- Subheadings: smaller type, underlined, italicized, capitalized, set in from margin

 SAMPLE TEXT AT RANDOM
- Read the first sentence of each paragraph.
- Read the last sentence of each paragraph.
- Note boldface or italic words (vocabulary or important words)
- Try to spot definitions, listings of items, pictures, diagrams, graphs, etc.

129

TEXTBOOK MARKING

Below are some suggestions for how to mark or signal what is important in a reading selection. The best method is to mark directly in the text. However, this sometimes is not possible if the book does not belong to you. Taking brief notes on another sheet of paper will do.

There is always the tendency to underline or write too much information. Usually, 10 percent of what you read needs to be underscored or marked. Noting significant ideas and details is an active, selective process.

Read the entire paragraph first before you mark anything. This allows you to see the concept presented and look back on what is important. Use a highlighting pen to mark words, phrases and passages, or identify main ideas and details in the margins by using a system of abbreviations or symbols (•, ?, , etc.) or by numbering (1, 2, 3, etc.).

Mark important material such as...
- titles and subtitles
- concepts on how titles/subtitles relate to each other (comparisons or contrasts, similarities)
- italicized/boldface words
- definitions and meanings
- examples
- lists (be sure to include the heading)
- main ideas (look for first and last sentences in paragraphs)

IN SUMMARY: <u>UNDERLINE</u>
- the right amount of information
- systematically and consistently
- accurately so it reflects the content of the reading material/selection

"Brain power" is significantly increased with the use of some type of "power reading strategy" or method. Like a finely tuned machine, your mind will work much more efficiently and effectively with a warm-up, rev-up, pace and cool-down plan.

When you consistently reuse a successful method of study, your brain becomes accustomed to a specific pattern; therefore, you are able to increase your time effectiveness. By making a regular habit of successful study habits such as power reading strategies, studying should take less effort and time and should produce more focused, quality results. These results are more likely to be permanent in your memory.

Be willing to give the following power reading strategy a try for three weeks and see if it doesn't really make a difference!

I. WARM-UP

A. Prepare your "gear":
1. Paper
2. Pencil
3. Dictionary
4. Texts
5. Notes

B. Prepare your surroundings:
1. Make sure there is good lighting.
2. Find a place that is relatively quiet.
3. Sit in a comfortable chair.
4. Listen to low/soft/slow music:
   a. To facilitate reading
   b. About 60 beats per minute is best

C. Prepare your mind:
1. Read to remember.
2. Eliminate distractions.

D. Review/reread the assignment for clarity.
1. Refresh your memory.
2. Determine your purpose for reading.
3. Set/focus your mind on desired objectives and outcomes.
4. Break down a complex reading assignment into reasonable "blocks."
   a. Use paper clips or rubber bands to separate sections.
   b. Consider subject headings/subheadings.
   c. Work backwards; consider the amount of time needed for completion and divide accordingly.

 Adapted from a presentation by Peggy Isakson. Used by permission.
© 1990 by Incentive Publications, Inc., Nashville, TN.

E. **Survey the material to be read:**
1. Use SQ3R system (see pages 136-138).
2. Reflect on what you already know:
    a. Relationships of material presented in class to the concepts in the text
    b. New material presented in the text not covered in class
    c. Main ideas
    d. Emphasized concepts
3. Identify what's important — find the main ideas.

II. STRETCH YOUR IMAGINATION

A. **Visualize yourself doing the work.**

B. **Form questions in your mind and read for the answers.**

C. **Continually link concepts, ideas and information with what you already know.**

D. **After reading several paragraphs:**
1. Close the book.
2. Recite from memory what you just read.

E. **Take ownership of the material by relating it to your own emotions, experiences and beliefs.**

III. CONSIDER YOUR PACE

A. **Choose your pace according to your purpose.**
1. Review "Five Different Reading Rates" (page 121).
2. Review "Types Of Paragraphs" (pages 123-124).
3. Become involved in your reading and set your purpose at the beginning.
4. It's more effective/efficient to read groups of words and short phrases for ideas rather than reading word-by-word.

Adapted from a presentation by Peggy Isakson. Used by permission.
© 1990 by Incentive Publications, Inc., Nashville, TN.

5. Continue to read when you come to unfamiliar words.
   a. It slows you down to look up words at this time.
   b. You lose your "train of thought."
   c. Often you can derive meaning through context clues.
6. Look up unfamiliar words after finishing the paragraph.
   a. Flag the word or write it on a 3" x 5" card.
   b. Write a brief definition.

B. Focus/concentrate 30-45 minutes per reading session.

C. Take a 10-15 minute break to do something active.

IV. **PUMP YOUR MIND**

A. Stretch/walk around to give you "thinking power" energy.

B. When your mind gets "off track":
   1. Make a check with a pencil on a piece of scratch paper.
      a. This causes you to refocus your thinking.
      b. Try to make fewer checks during the next reading block.
   2. Invent images as you read.
   3. Use your fingers to "guide" over subject headings.
   4. Talk to yourself while skimming and scanning if possible.

C. While reading:
   1. Read favorite/easier materials first — then more difficult materials.
   2. If your purpose is to take notes:
      a. Select and consistently use one method of note-taking.
      b. Read the information in short "blocks" that deal with the same topic, then quickly reread the information and take notes.
         c. Take complete notes (but only necessary notes) and include:
            1. Vocabulary words/definitions
            2. Words/phrases in italics

 Adapted from a presentation by Peggy Isakson. Used by permission.
© 1990 by Incentive Publications, Inc., Nashville, TN.

   3. Important names, dates, places
   4. Causes/effects
   5. Relationships between/among concepts
   6. Listed items
   7. Chapter headings, subheadings and important supporting details
   8. Important information from charts, graphs, tables
   9. Note that supplement and add to your class notes
  3. Construct a mind map.
     a. Continue to add to it as you read.
     b. Actively organize your thoughts about the assignment.

 D. Use a system to "flag" concepts (by paragraphs):
   1. Color-code ideas or write in margins where possible.
     a. Green or U = understand
     b. Yellow or C = confusing
     c. Red or D = don't understand
   2. Use a pencil to write a code in the margins, and erase when you have finished with the text (for textbooks in which you cannot write).

V. COOL DOWN AND REVIEW

 A. Sit back and relax for two minutes and recite the main ideas aloud.

 B. Choose/use a memory technique/mnemonic device.

 C. Share ideas with family or friends.

 D. Construct:
   1. Study sheets
   2. 3" x 5" cards
   3. Graphic organizers (mind maps)

Adapted from a presentation by Peggy Isakson. Used by permission.
© 1990 by Incentive Publications, Inc., Nashville, TN.

SQ3R

There are many study methods that can be used effectively and can be applied to textbook reading assignments. These methods are important and can save you time in the long run because they give you an overall view of the content as well as focus your mind on the purpose at hand.

You can gain much by understanding main ideas and concepts from the very beginning. Prereading exercises (such as "Survey" and "Question") as well as ending exercises (such as "Recite" and "Review") result in increased reading rates and comprehension. Finding, understanding and applying main ideas and supporting details are much easier when a "power reading" approach is utilized. Also, committing information to memory is aided by such a systematic approach.

Having a "plan of attack" or study method that is used on a regular basis will guarantee success.

SQ3R was originally developed by Francis P. Robinson. It has been thoroughly researched, tested and widely used as one of the best study skills for textbook reading. Using it the first time may prove to be a little time-consuming. However, as you continue to apply it, you'll find it to be one of the most efficient and effective study skills for increasing your BRAIN POWER!

BOOKMOBILE

SURVEY
- Review the reading assignment.
- Read titles/subtitles.
- Notice words/phrases in italics or boldface type.
- Skim illustrations, charts, graphs and other visual devices.
- Determine the general idea of the overall content.
- Focus on main ideas.
- Read the final summary paragraph.
- Read any questions at the end of the chapter/selection.

QUESTION
- Turn main/sub topics in boldface type into questions (use *who, what, when, where or why*).
- Determine your reading rate and the number of times to read the selection.
- Take any unanswered questions to class after completing the reading assignment.

READ
- Actively read to answer the questions — become involved.
- Get details and supporting examples.
- Highlight, underline or write important facts after reading one section (study guides and mind maps are particularly helpful).
- Note sequence/order, if important.
- Visualize as you read — make it real.

RECITE
- At the end of each section, stop to silently or orally answer original questions.
- For long-term understanding, recite aloud.
- Use your own words.
- Jot down cue phrases.
- Quiz yourself immediately on what you've just studied.

REVIEW
- If you cannot recite main ideas/details of each section, reread it.
- Relate one section of the reading assignment to another to develop a whole picture.
- Write a summary, including main ideas (construct a mind map or other graphic organizer).
- Make a study guide/sheet.
- Review again within 24 hours, then again within 72 hours, and twice more within the week.

SQ3R Chart

Use this "check-off chart" to monitor your SQ3R practice. Use it consistently until it becomes a habit. You should see a decrease in "amount of time spent" each time you use the SQ3R chart. Give it a try — you won't regret it!

Assignment:	Due Date ___ Amount of time spent ___ Class ___	Due Date ___ Amount of time spent ___ Class ___	Due Date ___ Amount of time spent ___ Class ___	Due Date ___ Amount of time spent ___ Class ___	Due Date ___ Amount of time spent ___ Class ___	Due Date ___ Amount of time spent ___ Class ___	Due Date ___ Amount of time spent ___ Class ___	Due Date ___ Amount of time spent ___ Class ___	Due Date ___ Amount of time spent ___ Class ___	Due Date ___ Amount of time spent ___ Class ___
SURVEY										
QUESTION										
READ										
RECITE										
REVIEW										

IMPORTANT COMPREHENSION SKILLS

Ask yourself the following questions to know if you have comprehended your reading assignment.

COMPREHENSION — a summary; the capacity for understanding and gaining knowledge.

1. Can I make good sense of the information?

2. Can I summarize the information in my own words and give it a title?

3. Did my reading rate match my purpose?

4. What was the main idea? Can I find a general statement supported by details?

5. Can I recite any details? How do they fit into the whole?

6. Is there anything I don't understand?

7. Can I identify and define the vocabulary in context? How does it relate to the topic?

8. Can I draw any conclusions from the information presented? How does this relate to…?

9. Do I understand the sequence in which the events occurred? How does one concept build upon another?

10. Can I make an inference based on the given facts?

11. Can I predict an outcome?

12. Can I recognize the author's tone of the message he/she is trying to get across?

MEDICINE

READING GRAPHICS

Knowing how to "read" graphic illustrations such as charts, tables and graphs is a matter of following a few steps. Keep in mind that the purpose of graphics is to demonstrate comparisons/contrasts, changes, trends, outcomes or explanations.

Try this easy approach:

1. **Read the title, subtitle, heading or subheading.**
   - helps focus your mind on the purpose
   - gives overview of information

2. **Read directional words/phrases on all sides.**
   - introduces/explains the vocabulary
   - provides directions and explanations
   - gives information as to what units the chart represents (time, money, mathematical units, etc.)

3. **Read the graphic illustration.**
   - watch for details, relationships
   - be aware of codes (numerical, color, symbols)
   - be aware of the general, overall concept

4. **Draw conclusions.**
   - predict patterns
   - analyze relationships
   - note what caused the change, increase, decrease
   - predict the next step (not shown) on the graph
   - study how each part fits into the whole

WHAT SLOWS YOU DOWN–AND HOW TO IMPROVE

REASONS FOR POOR READING	HELPFUL SOLUTIONS
1. Lack of purpose	1. Intend to "read to learn." Use SQ3R. Refer to "Determining Reading Purpose" (page 119).
2. Inappropriate reading rate	2. Be flexible according to your specific purpose — refer to "Five Different Reading Rates" (page 121).
3. Poor vision	3. Have your eyes checked by a doctor.
4. Eye stress/strain	4. Have your eyes checked by a doctor. Check for appropriate lighting. Rest your eyes periodically. Clean your glasses. Get up and walk around. Don't bend your neck. Hold your book upright at a proper distance.
5. Regressive reading (Rereading words and sentences over and over.)	5. Train your eyes to move ahead smoothly at a fixed pace and rhythm. Use your finger or index card if you have to for a short period of time.

REASONS FOR POOR READING	HELPFUL SOLUTIONS
6. **Inappropriate eye movement** (Skip words/phrases; skip lines or focus on wrong line)	6. Use your finger or 3″ x 5″ card to help your eyes track. Do not make this a habit, but use it only to establish an eye movement pattern.
7. **Pronouncing words as you read** (In your mind with your "inner voice" or whisper reading)	7. Try to read faster than you can internally or verbally say the words. Read blocks or phrases of words instead of single words. If you whisper, read with a pencil between your lips; when it falls out, you'll be reminded of your habit.
8. **Word-by-word reading** (Too slow)	8. Train your eyes to "see" phrases instead of single words: • begin slowly by widening your visual "spread" to group words • make a conscious effort to pace yourself • keep increasing the length to include many words Try to force your eyes to move smoothly and rhythmically instead of jerking. • listen to a clock tick and pace yourself

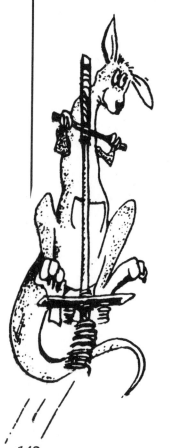

continued

REASONS FOR POOR READING	HELPFUL SOLUTIONS
9. **Lack of concentration** (Daydreaming)	9. Record your concentrated reading time and consistently try to increase it. Have a positive attitude that you can improve. When you notice your mind wandering, make a check mark on a piece of paper to refocus your thoughts. Try to decrease the number of marks per reading time.
10. **Lack of confidence**	10. Stop thinking of yourself as a slow or poor reader. Know and believe that there are many new ways you can try to improve. Have patience with yourself. Make reading a natural habit. Convince yourself that reading will become easier and more fun with practice. Brainstorm what you already know about the topic before you begin reading it. Know that there is important information to be gained from reading the assignment.

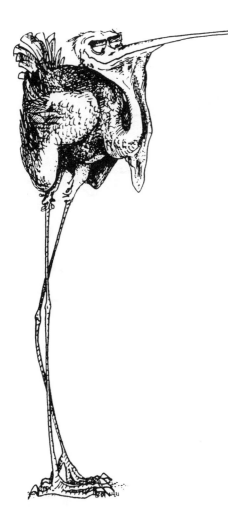

REASONS FOR POOR READING	HELPFUL SOLUTIONS
11. Poor posture	11. Sit up and do not bend your neck. Use proper position angle and distance for books.
12. Moving your head instead of your eyes to read	12. Cup your chin with your hand and put your elbow on the table/desk. When you feel your head move, it will remind you of your habit.

"The urge to do comes only from doing..."

HINTS FOR EFFECTIVE READING

1. Know your purpose before you read.

2. Read to remember.

3. Skip what you don't need or want to read.

4. Read for ideas when appropriate.

5. It's better to read for the knowledge of the information rather than for decoding skills (sounding out words one-by-one).

6. Read the first and last sentence of each paragraph for main ideas and summary.

7. Question while you read and read to answer the questions.

8. Guess where/what the author is trying to tell you.

9. Have a plan for how to read the subject matter.

10. Read the questions at the end of the chapter or section first. They usually reflect/signal the main ideas of the material to be read.

DID YOU KNOW...

- After a single reading, the average student forgets 80% of what he or she has read.

- Research has shown that students who spend 25% of their time reading and 75% of their time reciting what they have read retain much more of the information than those who spend 100% of their time reading.

WHEN THE READING IS HARD

TRY THESE:

1. Reread the material.

2. Change your surroundings, move around, and become physically active.

3. Try listening to soft, quiet music with 60 beats per minute.

4. Try to visualize and feel the concept or information.

5. Build and understand the paragraph by reading one sentence at a time.

6. Build and understand the reading assignment by fully comprehending one paragraph before moving on to the next.

7. Form a study group.

8. Read the material aloud and in front of a mirror if possible.

9. Decrease your reading rate.

10. Summarize at the end of each paragraph by writing or reciting.

11. Discuss the material with a family member or friend.

12. Put the book down for awhile and return to it in thirty minutes.

13. Ask the teacher for help or get a tutor.

14. Pretend that you understand the material and try to teach it to someone else.

15. Look up alternative references in the library.

MEMORY

Focus On Memory

1. Link whatever you're trying to learn with what you already know.

2. Intend to remember when you learn.

3. Use mnemonics that work for you.

4. Colors, shapes, placement and pictures are important to your memory.

5. Get past short-term memory and learn for long-term memory.

6. Make your memorizing methods organized.

7. Be smart, work with your memory and not against it.

8. Make remembering a habit.

9. Clarify, categorize, organize and review information for better memory.

10. Break up material in small units and review daily.

YOUR MEMORY

Your mind is built to remember. It never forgets or loses anything throughout your entire life. We say we "forget" when actually we have lack of recall due to memory blocks or the misplacement of information.

It is a natural tendency to remember only those things or concepts with which we agree or deem important. We simply pay more attention to the ideas and information we intend to remember or relate to our own priorities.

There are many techniques, strategies, mnemonics and tricks which can enable you to memorize and recall almost anything. First, you must intend to remember and learn the information and then set a realistic goal. Like most any aspect of your life, if you focus your concentration and intent upon re-membering, you will succeed. Real-ize that you can improve your memo-ry. Don't waste time making excuses or blaming yourself. Use that time to your own advantage!

1. **THERE ARE THREE BASIC PROCESSES INVOLVED IN MEMORY:**

   encoding – the process of readying information for storage
   storage   – the saving of information for use in the future - memory
   retrieval – recalling information from storage - continuous process

2. **THERE ARE SIX TYPES OF MEMORY:**

   Sensory Memory: fleeting impressions usually involving the five senses

   - taste
   - sound
   - smell
   - feel
   - sight

   Motor Skill Memory: usually involving physical movement

   - riding a bicycle
   - swimming

   Verbal/Semantic Memory: usually involving language

   - associated with the meaning of words or mathematical symbols

   Photographic Memory: remembering visual information

   - picture memory
   - usually lasts only a short period of time

Types
of
Memory

Short-Term Memory: temporary storage of selected memory items; any thoughts/experiences in the mind at any specific point in time

- spelling words for the week
- melodies to popular songs
- license plate numbers
- cramming for a test

Long-Term Memory: usually permanent storage of large amounts of material; unlimited in capacity for indefinite periods of time

- your name, address, etc.
- decoding skills that enable you to read
- birthdays
- foreign languages

3. **FACTORS IMPORTANT FOR RESTORING INFORMATION IN LONG-TERM MEMORY:**

- intend to remember
- how meaningful the information is to you
- organization of the information
- linking with previous knowledge
- spaced learning blocks
- mnemonic strategies
- integration of the five senses

1. Learning stays with you. In order to forget something, you first have to learn it. You can't forget anything you don't learn or understand.

2. The human mind can remember five to seven unrelated ideas for a short time.

3. It takes about 15 to 25 minutes of practice over several days to successfully memorize and retain information.

4. Freud concluded that motivation, desire and emotion play a large part in your "brain power."

5. With the exceptions of disease, injury and death, the brain never forgets anything. Only our inability to recall stands in our way.

6. The average adult cannot remember 50% of what he or she has just read. Twenty-four hours later, recall is about 20%. Quick and constant review is the remedy.

7. For right-handed people, visual information is processed in the right hemisphere of the brain, and verbal information is processed in the left hemisphere. If you make up a picture to go with material to be processed, it is then implanted in both hemispheres. This increases the chances of recall.

8. At least 40% of total learning time should be spent reviewing new information.

9. Adult attention spans average from 10 to 30 minutes.

10. We forget new information rapidly at first (if not rehearsed or practiced). Then the rate of forgetfulness "levels off" over time.

11. Brain research suggests that information or thoughts create paths in the memory. These consistent paths are called neural traces. By using and reusing the information through review, these paths are deepened which allows for easier and quicker recall of the information.

12. Effective memory is the ability to produce the right information at the right time.

13. Your brain remembers:

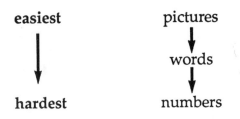

easiest   pictures

↓   words

hardest   numbers

14. An effective memory:

- increases your adaptability and creativity
- finds relationships between new information and what is known
- improves with consistent use
- is essential to learning

15. Most of us forget more than 99% of the phone numbers we learn and more than 90% of the names of the people we meet.

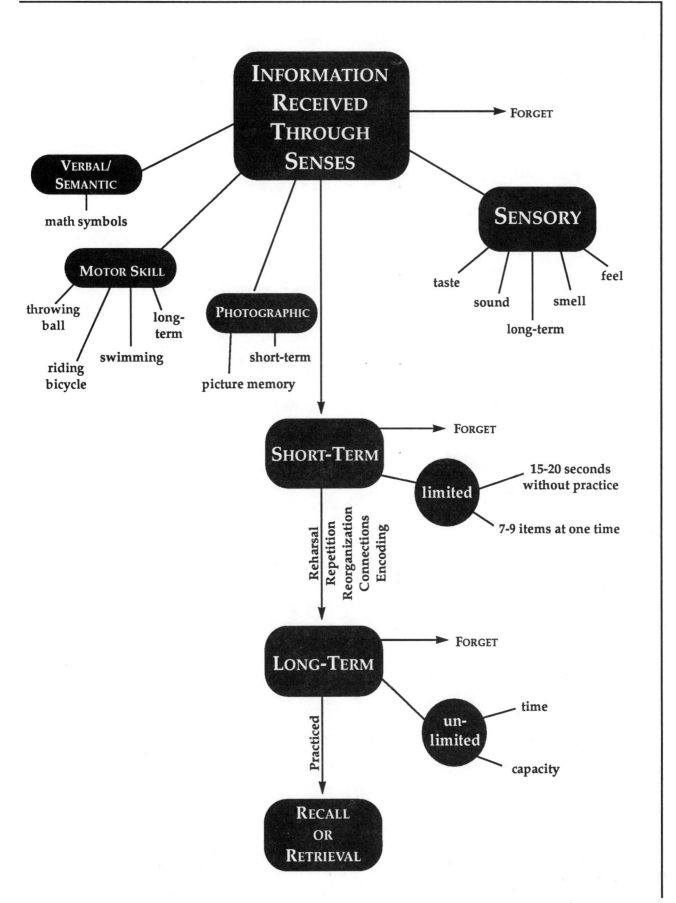

Don't Bury Yourself in Excuses

I. INTEND TO REMEMBER

A. Become an active learner.
1. Create an interest for yourself.
   a. Talk with others.
   b. Get outside help.
   c. Read critically.
   d. Anticipate/predict outcomes or the sequence of events.
   e. Make connections with known information.
   f. See relationships.
   g. Integrate the new idea with previous learning.
2. Be sure your mind stores the information your eyes see.

B. Be positive.
1. You create your own boredom.
2. Your attitude can unlock your ability to recall.
3. Tell yourself "I will remember this!"
4. New learning can be frustrating. Be tolerant of yourself and the material.

C. Pay attention by asking yourself:
1. "How do I remember?"
2. "What techniques/methods already are successful?"
3. "What do I remember about this?"
4. "What's important about this?"
5. "How will I use this?"

D. Work with your memory — not against it.
1. Relax to allow better recall.
2. Let go of tension-blocking devices.
   a. Try to recall information related to blocked thought.
   b. Create visual images.

II. ORGANIZE

A. Understand the material well.

B. Decide how much to memorize at one time.

C. Decide on memory strategy (mnemonics).

D. Categorize material into meaningful units.

E. Associate the material with other learned material.

F. Learn from the general to the specific.

III. SET A GOAL TO LEARN AND REMEMBER

A. Relate the information to your needs and goals — make it meaningful.

B. Be realistic.

C. Intend to apply the information to your life and make it familiar and comfortable to use.

IV. SCHEDULE YOUR STUDY TIME

A. Memory study is best distributed over several short periods/blocks of time to increase the amount of recall.

B. Study the hardest material during prime study time.

V. DECIDE TO IMPROVE YOUR CONCENTRATION

A. Eliminate distractions by considering:
1. The place you study
2. The time of day you study
3. Your physical condition
4. Background noise

B. Focus your attention by:
1. Setting a specific goal
2. Timing yourself
3. Becoming interested
4. Varying the use of your skills and the difficulty of the material/subjects
5. Finding a specific point of interest (watch, ring, fingers) to stare at while recalling/retrieving information
6. Keeping a distractions list
   a. Add any distractions that break your concentration.
   b. Continually work toward reducing items on the list.
7. Giving yourself rewards consistently and appropriately

I. **WHEN TO REVIEW**

   A. Review after class to reinforce short-term memory.

   B. Review that evening just before going to sleep (uses the subconscious to continue processing information and aids long-term memory).

   C. Review while editing your notes (within 24 hours).

   D. Review each day thereafter for 10 minutes each time.

   E. Review again in one month — immediately before going to sleep

   F. Continually quiz yourself and try to relate previously learned materials to current studies.

II. **USE WHAT YOU REMEMBER**

   A. **Apply the information.**
      1. Continually relate the new information with the known information.
      2. If a portion of the information gets blocked from recall, retrieving associated material will often unblock the wanted information.

III. "OVERLEARN" THE MATERIAL

    A. Continue to review after you know the information.

    B. Use the buddy system — find another student in your class with whom to discuss the material.

IV. REWARD YOURSELF

    A. Compliment yourself on a job well-done.

    B. Learn to trust your memory — it is your best resource.

Make Remembering A Habit...

PRACTICE!

Mnemonic strategies are memory aids that provide a systematic approach for organizing and remembering facts that have no apparent link or connection of their own. Mnemonics provide the tools necessary to memorize and recall almost any information. "Forgetting" (lack of recall) occurs rapidly unless certain steps are taken to process the material into memory. Mnemonics can provide the pathway for those steps with fun and ease.

HINTS FOR USING MNEMONICS:
Apply *all* of your senses to the active process of learning and combine them whenever possible.

- **Get physical**
  - orally recite whenever possible
  - write the information several times
  - walk/pace if you need to while reciting, reading, etc.
  - gesture with your hands or face, if it helps

- **Visualize**
  - form clear pictures in your mind
  - the mind remembers pictures more easily and for longer periods than words

- **Link information**
  - hook new information onto old information
  - group or chunk material together
  - remember similar/associated material when memory is blocked (serves to "jog" memory)

MEMORY TIPS
- **Match material to be learned with the most effective memory technique/mnemonic device.**

- **Combine memory techniques whenever possible (doubles the chances of long-term memory).**

- **Always repeat orally as you write.**

- **Use 3" x 5" cards.**
  - one entry per card
  - place card in upper left corner of mirror, bulletin board, locker, etc.

MNEMONICS/STRATEGIES FOR IMPROVING MEMORY

STRATEGY	DEFINITION	EXAMPLE
Mind Map	Organize mental maps from known information; then fill in missing information: main ideas, details, categories/parts, diagram labels.	government — president, congress, supreme court; Bush, Senate, House, Warren
Visual Chains	A visual cycle of pictures and/or words: cause/effect, linking systems, sequencing.	O → ← CO_2 cycle
Acronyms	Let the first letter of each word in a sentence represent the first letter of the words/list you wish to memorize: lists, sequencing.	H—Huron O—Ontario M—Michigan E—Erie S—Superior
Word Links	Use the meaning of one word to associate with another: definitions, pairs.	The capitol of Oregon is Salem. (Think: There are many sailboats in Oregon because it's on the ocean. What do you do with these boats? Sail-em.)
Poems, Rhymes Nonsense Verses, Lyrics	Using a familiar tune, substitute information to be learned: details, sequencing.	"Mary Had A Little Lamb" "The ABC Song" In 1492, Columbus sailed the ocean blue.

continued

STRATEGY	DEFINITION	EXAMPLE
Take-A-Trip	Visualize familiar objects around a room and attach some information/word with each object: lists.	dresser desk books bed
Acrostics	Make up a sentence using the first letter of each word: sequencing, lists.	<u>E</u>very <u>G</u>ood <u>B</u>oy <u>D</u>oes <u>F</u>ine. (musical scale)
Picture Objects	Using a familiar object, associate information around it: lists, details.	Picture your finger. To learn prepositions, think of the action involved (around, to, from, etc.).
Hookups	Using one word or series of letters, "hook up" information beginning with the same letter: details, categories/parts, lists.	N — New Mexico, North Carolina, Nevada A — Alabama, Alaska, Arkansas T — Texas, Tennessee
Make A Tape	Make a tape recording of information to be learned: vocabulary, foreign languages, spelling, lists, sequences, almost anything.	Play it repeatedly over several days. Play it just before sleeping at night.
Write It!	Write it repeatedly and say it aloud as you write: almost anything.	Write it just before you go to sleep.

MNEMONICS/STRATEGIES FOR IMPROVING MEMORY

continued

STRATEGY	DEFINITION	EXAMPLE
Numbers	Write the numbers to be remembered: sequences.	Notice a special sequence and associate it with some familiar date. (birthday) 2 17 64 mo. day year
Poetry	The best way to remember poetry is to break it into small, meaningful sections.	Remember the story. Practice the meter/rhythm.
Sayings	Link information with a famous saying and substitute words.	A penny saved is... No pencil is as sharp as...
Mental Pictures	Visualize how you see or expect to see a total picture: diagrams.	Close your eyes and visualize an X-ray view of the skeleton from the head down (skeletal labeling).
Create An Experience	Mentally and visually create/recall an experience and link information to be learned with what you do: sequences, details.	Imagine yourself making cookies, building a bookshelf, etc., step-by-step. Plug information to be learned into each step.

STEPS TO AID MEMORY

1. Clarify – fully understand what it is you want to learn and memorize.

2. Motivate – intend to learn, remember and concentrate on the new information; develop a strong, realistic purpose; clearly choose to remember.

3. Categorize – define the information to be learned and its intended purpose; choose between short and long-term memory storage.

4. Organize – group information so that main ideas and details are connected; relate new information to known material.

5. Plan – select the best strategy/technique to fit the material and need.

6. Review – repeat the information, combining as many of the five senses as possible; make it a habit.

MEMORY BLOCKERS are any factors that interfere with your ability to recall facts.

WHY DO WE FORGET?

- lack of intentional purpose to remember

- faulty recall system

- poor listener

- lack of attention

- too painful or embarrassing

- lack of preparation

- tired

- cannot recall because of misplaced data in the memory

- fear

- critical of information

- jump to conclusions

- physical stress

- distracted

- bored

- dislike the person or disagree with what he or she says

- lack of understanding

- mental stress or strain

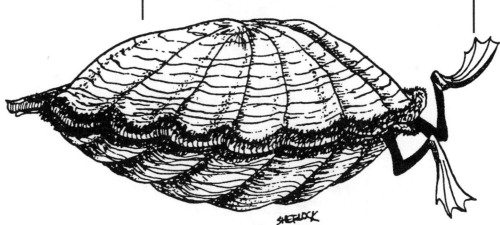

HOW TO STUDY A FOREIGN LANGUAGE

All languages have certain common aspects. No language is completely "foreign." You should apply many memory strategies to understand and remember what you read and hear. Learning to think in the language is the ultimate goal. This includes speaking and reading fluently and refraining from "translating words into English and then back again."

Learning a second language is not as difficult as it may seem if it is approached in a systematic, organized and persistent manner. Use the following steps to achieve success!

I.   **SET YOUR GOALS**

    A. To think in the language, first try to:
       1. Read it and translate it into your own language.
       2. Understand the spoken language.
       3. Speak it.

    B. Keep up with daily assignments.

    C. Review over and over again.

II. IDENTIFY YOUR STRENGTHS AND WEAKNESSES IN LEARNING A FOREIGN LANGUAGE

(Write S for strength and W for weakness.)

A. _____ reading the language
B. _____ understanding the spoken language
C. _____ composing thoughts in the language
D. _____ keeping up with new vocabulary
E. _____ translating
F. _____ writing the language

III. RECOGNIZE COMMON PROBLEMS

A. Lack an understanding of English grammar.

B. Fall behind on assignments.
   1. Vocabulary (memorization and spelling)
   2. Reading assignments
   3. Grammar study
      a. Forget basic English grammar
      b. Do not understand grammatical terms
      c. Do not understand idioms

IV. PROGRESSIVE STEPS IN LEARNING:

A. Master one level and then move on to the next one.
   1. Learn the meanings of words (various forms/tenses).
   2. Learn simple phrases/sentences (idioms).
   3. Master word order (the relationships of words in clauses or sentences).
   4. Pronounce words or translate them in complex sentences.
   5. Think in the language.

USING YOUR SENSES

Think of all of the senses you used as a child to learn your first language. Did you listen to those around you in order to learn vocabulary? Did you imitate their sounds by speaking? Did you decode the strange symbols in books in order to learn the meanings of printed words, phrases and sentences? Did you try to recreate your own stories by writing? Of course you did! So it is with any language. You can use these same methods to learn a second language. By repeating these important steps, you can build your memory so that it will function in a foreign language. With practice and persistence, the language soon will cease to be "foreign"!

LISTENING

1. Ask yourself this question: "How did I first learn English?" Understand that listening comes first.

2. Intend to listen with the aim of repeating what you hear.

3. Look up the pronunciation guide in your book.

4. Listen for:
   - The sounds of words and how they flow together
   - The meanings of words in phrases

5. Use any or all listening aids available.
   - Use listening labs at school.
   - Make your own tapes.
   - Check out tapes from the library/media center.
   - Go to foreign films.
   - Watch educational T V language courses.
   - Listen to foreign students talk.

SPEAKING

1. **Intend to speak the language and to use it as often as possible.**
   - In the beginning, expect to be slow and to mispronounce words and use words incorrectly.
   - To form a good habit, immediately correct any mistakes.

2. **Emphasize recitation.**
   - This is especially important.
   - Spend 80% of your time on this.
   - Practice, practice, practice!

3. **Learn grammar correctly.**
   - Why learn grammar?
     - It makes the language "second nature."
     - It helps you to construct your own sentences.
     - It helps you understand what others say and write.

4. **Helpful Hints:**
   - Know how to use and apply memorized lists of detached words.
   - Use dictionaries.
   - Attach some real meaning to your memorizing.
   - Whenever you don't understand a new grammatical term, ask the teacher or look up the term.
   - Be sure to memorize the exceptions to the rules and recite them in phrases and sentences.

READING

1. Intend to become proficient in understanding written material.
2. Use the text.
    *   Look for notes regarding reading assignments.
    *   Be familiar with resources in the text such as the glossary or dictionary in the back of the book.
3. Try to read the entire assignment the first time without translating it.
    *   Use context clues.
4. Try to rapidly progress from word-to-word translation to an understanding of complete phrases and sentences.
5. Always reread a passage soon after translating it.
6. Break unknown words into their elements and determine the meaning of the elements.
    *   root words, affixes, prefixes
7. Learn "cognate" words (words that have a common heritage).
8. Read aloud when possible.
    *   Hear yourself speak the language.
    *   Work toward fluency and expression.

WRITING

1. Intend to learn to write the language correctly and easily.
2. Write in phrases at first.
    *   Write your thoughts as you think them.
3. Pay attention to spelling, word order/form and irregularities.
4. Proofread your writing by reading it aloud.

TEST-TAKING SKILLS

Focus On

Test-Taking Skills

1. Improve test grades by becoming testwise.

2. Recognize test anxiety and turn it into positive energy.

3. Make appropriate study time for tests.

4. Form a study group.

5. Compile and edit class/text notes and handouts into useful study sheets.

6. Always ask the teacher about the test format a few days before the test.

7. Become familiar with intelligent guessing strategies.

8. Review specifics on how to take each type of test.

9. Know how to use your time wisely during the test.

10. Know essay direction words and how to interpret them.

Becoming "Testwise"

In order to do well on a test, you must know the subject matter as well as how to take the test. Knowing how to demonstrate your full potential and the knowledge that you have learned is called "testwiseness." Your intelligence and previous knowledge combined with new information that you learn in preparation for tests should result in your ability to perform well and succeed. The following pages will give you numerous strategies to apply before, during and after taking a test. Research indicates that as many as twenty points can be gained simply by using good "testwiseness" tools.

Using your study time effectively to prepare for a test is a key factor in taking tests. Your approach to studying will be determined by the type of test. Basically, there are two types of exams: objective (multiple-choice, true/false, matching, fill-in-the-blank) and subjective (essay). Both of these "types" can be found in standardized as well as nonstandardized exams. Standardized tests are those that have established norms (the average achievement of a large group) which allow teachers to compare your score against the scores of other students. These tests often are given in booklet form to large groups and are used to predict your achievement and skills in certain areas. Some examples of standardized tests are:

1. **Achievement Tests** – cover many subjects; measure your knowledge level in the specific area

2. **Aptitude Tests** – predict your success in a course or program; often determine entrance and placement by colleges, SAT tests

3. **Diagnostic Tests** – show strengths and weaknesses in a specific subject area; often determine placement of level in a particular subject

Nonstandardized tests do not have norms and usually are the tests most teachers give to "gauge" a student's knowledge. Such tests usually are constructed by the teacher and are taken by the student. The remainder of this chapter will deal with non-standardized tests and how to prepare for them and take them with success.

There are many important and critical aspects that lead to good test scores. Probably the most important are to intend to do well on the test and to have a positive mental attitude. Believing that you are capable of achieving the score you want is half the battle.

If you can understand that testing is an essential part of the learning process and that you actually can learn from tests, you are that much ahead of the game. This also can aid you in learning how to control test anxiety and direct negative energy into a positive channel. Recognizing that tests do not always measure what you learn and that some teachers make poor tests should help you to be kind to yourself when your test results are lower than you anticipate. If you rely on thorough knowledge of the subject matter, commonsense and learned test-taking skills, you can relax and expect success when taking a test!

Studying, understanding and applying the following information about how to become "testwise" could possibly raise your test scores for years to come. It definitely will make you a more relaxed and successful student!

REASONS FOR POOR PERFORMANCE ON TESTS

- absent from school and didn't make up the work
- didn't pay attention (listen) in class
- didn't do homework
- didn't care
- didn't read text
- waited too long to begin studying
- wasn't organized
- didn't get enough sleep
- studied wrong material
- changed too many answers
- poor attitude about the subject
- didn't review from day-to-day
- cramming was ineffective
- didn't budget time to study
- overconfident
- test anxiety
- memory block during testing
- think the teacher is unfair
- don't like the teacher
- lack of testwiseness
- ran out of time
- didn't check answers
- left too many answers blank

WAYS TO AVOID THESE

1. Keep up with your studies.
2. Learn good study habits and apply them.
3. Train your memory.
4. Become testwise.
5. Be positive.
6. Be organized.

TEST ANXIETY ... AND HOW TO FREE YOURSELF

Grades, grades, grades! A test grade reflects how well you did on *that* particular test — it doesn't necessarily reflect your intelligence, how much you learned, your creativity, or your worth as a person. It's important to keep this in mind and to view test grades in proper perspective with the rest of your life.

If you have "butterflies" in your stomach before a test, don't be disturbed. Most people get them. A little extra "charge" or adrenaline can help you perform at your best. Turning that extra bit of energy into a positive attribute actually can increase your test score. However, real test anxiety can block your memory and prevent you from doing well. By understanding and accepting test anxiety and then applying successful tools to conquer it, you can overcome this barrier and practice effective test-taking strategies.

Carefully consider the test anxiety information on page 180 and try some of the suggestions the next time you find yourself becoming anxious.

SYMPTOMS OF TEST ANXIETY

- nervousness
- fear of…
    - forgetting
    - the unknown
    - not finishing the test
    - not studying the right
    - material
- nonstop talking
- withdrawal
- fidgeting
- dread

- self "put-down"
- lack of concentration
- change in appetite
- high degree of confusion
- nausea
- sweaty palms
- sleeplessness
- nosebleeds
- memory blocks
- increased and noticeable
    worry
- deep concern about a personal
    reflection on you
- extreme quietness
- inappropriate laughter
- extreme lack of patience
- anger
- boasting
- inadequate preparation

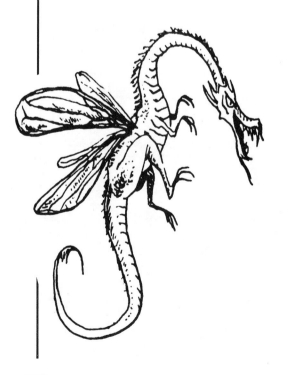

STRATEGIES TO STOP TEST ANXIETY

1. Stop Yourself

When you first have any negative thought, immediately begin positive "self-talk." This is the way in which you communicate with yourself "inside your head." Interrupt the continuous thoughts of worry by giving yourself permission to be concerned as you channel your energy into doing something to help yourself. Once you have admitted that you are anxious, accept it and continue trying to improve the situation. This focuses your attention on a positive action rather than on negative worry.

2. Plan Your Attack

Use some of these strategies as alternatives to nonproductive anxiety and worry. Be sure to try each strategy. You have everything to gain. Once you find several strategies that work for you, you can rely on them with great trust. Just knowing that you are in control of the situation and can handle your feelings will allow you to perform much better during the test.

Visualize   yourself studying in an organized manner and taking the test with success and ease. See the grade you want clearly written at the top of the paper. Include a lot of details and make the visualization very realistic. *See* your success in your mind. Visualizing is a very powerful instrument!

Daydream   about something you especially enjoy — a hobby, sport, vacation, certain location or time, someone special, etc. Make it a vivid dream with warm, comfortable surroundings.

Make Up   a story about anything preposterous. Blow it "up and out of reality" — exaggerate! Imagine the worst thing that could happen to you if you did poorly on the test. Make it funny and very unrealistic. Soon you will be laughing at yourself.

Recall   the helpful tools and methods you have learned and have come to trust. They will aid your memory. There are so many — and you can count on them whenever you want or need them.

Breathe by taking several slow, controlled, deep breaths. Concentrate on the movement of the air as it goes in and out of your body. Focus *all* of your attention on breathing!

Notice your body posture and any tense muscles. Make a conscious effort to relax those muscles. First, tense each muscle as much as possible for a few seconds and then relax it. Tell yourself that you are now relaxed. You may want to "relax" only those muscles that you can feel. Or, begin at the top of your body and work down to your toes. Focus your entire attention toward this effort.

Do Something physical, such as exercise (if the situation permits it).

HAVE SELF-CONFIDENCE!

PREPARATION BEFORE THE TEST

IN SCHOOL
- **Study the teacher for clues as to what's important:**
  - Voice (volume, inflection, speed changes)
  - Gestures (face, hand, body)
  - Materials (handouts, models, films, overhead transparencies)
  - Repetition of main ideas/details
  - Know the types of questions the teacher will ask (requests for details, general overview of the subject matter, objective or subjective tests, time sequencing, graphic information such as charts, graphs, maps, etc.).

- **In class...**
  - Intend to learn.
  - Listen carefully.
  - Take good notes and review them often.
  - Ask good questions, including what material is to be covered on the test and what form the test will take.
  - Try to condense and capture important ideas into a mind map or outline at the end of each class.

- **Get information from other students.**
  - Talk with others who have previously taken the class.
  - Get old tests.
    - Don't expect the exact same questions on the next test.
    - Look at the general concepts covered.
    - Look at the format (true/false, matching, multiple-choice, short answer, essay, etc.).
    - Watch for the amount of questions taken from class lectures, reading assignments, handouts, audiovisual aids and other assignments.
    - Look for trick questions.
    - Watch for the information that wasn't covered.
    - Did the test require recall of facts or reasoning skills?

AT HOME
- Refer to the note-taking strategies related to creating study sheets and the reading strategies in other chapters of this book.

- A few days before the test, list concepts you think are most important and ask the teacher, at a convenient time, if these are appropriate topics to study for the test.
  - Choose a time when the teacher has set aside a few moments to spend with individual students (after class, before school or after school are good).
  - This demonstrates to the teacher that you have taken the interest and initiative in studying for the test.
  - What have you got to lose? Most teachers will be very helpful and will be delighted that you have an interest in the class.

- Gather all of the study materials you will need.

- Review any class/reading notes, handouts, study sheets, 3" x 5" cards, texts, course outlines, out-of-class assignments, old tests, mind maps, etc.
  - Pay particular attention to:
    - Lists
    - Italicized or boldface words or phrases
    - Material "weighted" in class (concepts stressed by the teacher through repetition or amount of time given to a concept)

- Divide material into what you know well, what you need to review, what is unfamiliar, etc.
  - Color-code or label this material. For example:
    - A or green = know well
    - B or yellow = review
    - C or red = unfamiliar

- **Construct additional 3" x 5" cards which include:**
    - Vocabulary
    - Definitions
    - Formulas
    - Lists of causes/effects, pros/cons
    - Summaries of concepts (cue words and phrases)

    (Note: These are especially good for open-book tests!)

- **Turn chapter headings and subheadings within chapters into possible test questions.**
    - Make up questions about material in the text and your notes. Then answer the questions under time pressure.

- **Review specific note-taking techniques and rehearse your "plan of attack"** (*especially important for essay tests*).

- **Form a "study group."**

- **Quickly review the material just before going to sleep. Your subconscious will continue to "rehearse" the information.**

- **Get a full night's sleep before the test.**

- **Have the positive attitude that you've studied and will do well on the test.**

BE ORGANIZED!

Forming a Study Group

WHY

1. Reinforces what you already know.
2. Provides the opportunity to practice and review.
3. Allows you to meet other students and to enjoy constructive studying in a fun atmosphere.
4. Enables you to learn new information from others.
5. Promotes a better understanding of confusing or unknown concepts.
6. Allows for better coverage of the material to be learned.
7. You are more likely to study if others are counting on you.

HOW

1. Notice who's in your class (close in ability and motivation to match your expectations).
2. Find five to six interested students.
3. Contact the students to arrange a meeting time and place (plan only one to start).
4. In the first session:
   a. Exchange names and phone numbers.
   b. Set specific goals for the group with reasonable time lines.
   c. Discuss:
      – Review the instructor's teaching style.
      – Conduct an overview of the subject matter (skim through text, notes).
      – Discuss each member's particular interest in that topic (previous knowledge).
      – Assign each member an equal quantity of text pages/notes to cover in detail.
      – Discuss possible test questions.
5. Test each other.

6. Review any weak spots.
7. Make a "plan of action" for getting additional help if needed.
8. If the first session is effective, set up another session (if necessary).
    - Make sure every member has a clear set of goals for the next session.
    - Be certain that each member understands his or her particular assignment.
    - Honestly and tactfully discuss any problems that occurred during the first session.
    - Name a time and place for the next session and get a commitment to attend from each member.
    - Make sure that each member records the names and phone numbers of all of the members as well as the meeting times and places.

GENERAL HINTS

- *The library is a poor place to meet. It will stifle creative excitement because of the noise limits.*

- *Food and beverages add fun and excitement and serve as a refreshing break in the middle of the session.*

- *Allow enough time to accomplish your goals but not enough time to foster a gab session.*

- *Appoint an appropriate person to be in charge of keeping the group "on task."*

- *If holding more than one session, take turns in keeping any necessary records.*

- *Understand that everyone pays equally for any photocopying costs that might occur due to an exchange of notes or study sheets.*

- *Secure any necessary permission ahead of time for the meeting time and place. Parents usually don't like to be surprised.*

TEST-TAKING TOOLS

Be sure to "clear" all supplies with the teacher *before* the test.

In Class

- 2 - 3 sharpened pencils with good erasers
- eraser
- erasable pen with eraser
- writing paper
- scratch paper
- compass/protractor
- calculator
- small stapler or paper clips

Open-Book Tests In Class

- all of the above
- text(s)
- all notes and study sheets
- 3" x 5" cards
- dictionary

Take Home

- all of the above
- thesaurus
- other references (grammar/writing guides)
- magazine articles
- old tests

LIST OF "QUALIFIERS"

Watch for these "qualifying" words in test questions. They can be a real help or hindrance to your answers!

General (usually true)

seldom
generally
probably
most
often
some
sometimes
usually

Specific

always	everyone
all	true
never	false
none	negative
frequently	positive
more than	except
less than	including
neither	many
both	few
everybody	equal to
impossible	inequality
absolutely	equality
nobody	superior
no one	inferior
because	whole
only	part
must	specifically
weak	strong

 Whenever you read one of these words in test directions, questions or answers…

- circle the word to fix your attention on that word
- consider the question/answer very carefully

INTELLIGENT GUESSING STRATEGIES

The "Intelligent Guessing Strategies" on pages 191 - 194 should be used only as a last resort if you don't know the answer *and* if you are penalized for guessing. If the test scoring system does not deduct points for wrong answers, it is always better to guess than to leave questions unanswered. Be sure to find out if guessing is penalized before taking the test.

Always choose an answer or "fill in" the answer and flag it (circle the number, draw a star or question mark beside the question, etc.) so that you can quickly determine the questions that need special attention when you are checking/reviewing your test. Fill in the answer the first time instead of "skipping" it with the intention of returning. It is very possible that time might run out and you won't have the opportunity to return to the question. Use any extra time to recheck flagged questions.

Research indicates that appropriate and correct application of intelligent guessing techniques can raise test scores significantly. Learn the following strategies well and use them with care. Remember to apply them only as a last resort if your recall fails or if you are totally unfamiliar with the material.

Statements/ Words Most Likely To Be True	Statements/ Words Most Likely To Be False	Type of Test	Examples
The most "general" statement.		multiple-choice true/false	The poem *The Cemetery of Whales* by Yevgeny Yevtuschenko: a. is not translatable b. is basically a criticism of communism c. refers only to situations in Russia d. appeals only to Jewish people
	absolute statements	multiple-choice	It is always hot in August. Words that are absolute: all no one always only everybody must impossible never absolutely none nobody everyone
	unfamiliar/ unknown words and phrases	multiple-choice true/false	Any words that you don't recall seeing during your study time.
	humorous alternatives, insults, jokes	multiple-choice matching (if there are extras)	

Statements/ Words Most Likely To Be True	Statements/ Words Most Likely To Be False	Type of Test	Examples
The most complete statements		multiple-choice	When memorizing information: a. start the night before b. have a positive attitude and intend to remember c. gather all the information together d. cram
	If alternatives range in value, eliminate the two extremes.	multiple-choice	The population of Boulder is: a. 250,000 b. 85,000 c. 43,500 d. 10,000
"All of the above" choice		multiple-choice	When constructing study sheets for a test, include: a. reading notes b. class notes c. graphs d. all of the above
	Statements that contain reasons or qualifying answers	true/false multiple-choice	Paul did poorly on the test because he went to a movie the night before instead of studying. F because, except, not

Statements/ Words Most Likely To Be True	Statements/ Words Most Likely To Be False	Type of Test	Examples
The longest choice		multiple-choice	*The Great Gatsby*: a. exploits fidelity <u>b.</u> demonstrates the revenge of the down-trodden on the rich c. occurs in Minneapolis d. illustrates Southern hospitality
If two choices are opposite, choose one of them		multiple-choice	Sigmund Freud: <u>a.</u> developed the theory b. did not develop the theory of psycho-analysis c. always advised the psychoanalysis for his patients d. felt that therapy should be carried out in a sanitarium
	If two choices are nearly the same, choose neither one.	multiple-choice	The most important thing that Abraham Lincoln did politically was to: a. wield an axe b. split rails <u>c.</u> issue the Emancipation Proclamation d. be shot in the Ford Theater after the war

Statements/ Words Most Likely To Be True	Statements/ Words Most Likely To Be False	Type of Test	Examples
Answer in the middle, especially with the most words		multiple-choice	When you don't know the right answer, you should: a. leave it blank b. answer using testwise strategies and then flag it c. go to the next one

A CLOSER LOOK AT NEGATIVES

Negatives are words or prefixes that change the meaning to the opposite.

Common Negative Words	Common Negative Prefixes	
not	un	non
except	in	im
false	il	ir
	dis	

- Be especially alert to negatives in objective test questions.
- Sometimes it is helpful to circle the negative words and prefixes in questions and answers.

Double Negatives are statements which contain two negatives — usually one word and one prefix. Cross out both. Then, reread and answer.

Ex: He is ~~not un~~athletic.

Triple Negatives are statements which contain three negatives —usually one word and two prefixes. Cross out two of the negatives. Then, reread and answer.

Ex: It is ~~not un~~kind to be impatient.

THINGS YOU SHOULD KNOW ABOUT CRAMMING
- Use it as a last resort.
- Your recall of information is seriously limited to 1 - 2 days.
- Your learning and the amount of material you can cover are limited due to lack of time.
- The general scope and understanding of the subject is limited.
- It takes longer to learn information under pressure.

HOW TO CRAM IF YOU MUST:
1. Determine the course's purpose.
2. Quickly survey the material for a broad overview.
3. Specifically skim class notes and the text.
4. Decide on a few main areas upon which to focus (it is better to thoroughly know some main ideas with supporting details than to spend your limited time barely learning everything).
5. Pay attention to handouts, definitions, lists, italicized words, dates, formulas and names.
6. Make study sheets, mind maps or other graphic organizers.
7. Review, recite and memorize using mnemonic devices whenever possible.
8. Go into the test with the attitude that you will do well with what you were able to study.
9. Don't waste time on the questions you don't know — skip them.
10. Review and apply the "intelligent guessing strategies" when possible.

- **Arrive early enough to:**
  - Gather all needed materials.
  - Choose a quiet part of the room (a corner in the front of the room is best).
    - to avoid the distractions of those in front of you
    - to hear clearly any oral directions
    - to read the chalkboard better

  - **"Settle in" and get comfortable.**
    - Visit the restroom.
    - Clean your glasses (if you have any).
    - Get a drink of water.
    - Remove all distracting items from your desk.
    - Sit erect in the chair to stay alert.
    - Relax (breathe deeply, stretch, etc.).
  - Quickly glance through your study sheets for a last review, if you feel like it.

- **Don't talk to others about test material — it is too confusing!**

- **If you are totally unfamiliar with the test room and feel uncomfortable about taking the test there, it is a good idea to make a brief visit to the test room before the test date.**

- **Bring all of your previous experiences and learning with you. Trust your study skills and test-taking strategies!**

FOCUS ON CONCENTRATING AND HAVE A POSITIVE ATTITUDE!

USE YOUR TIME WISELY

1. Put your name on all pages of the test.

2. Think only positive thoughts.

3. Make a conscious effort to relax your neck, shoulders and upper back.

4. Write key words and phrases from any oral directions.

5. Don't start writing immediately. Look over the entire test to learn the number and kind of questions.

6. Budget your time; allow yourself time after you have finished the test to check your answers.

7. Read all directions twice. Circle key words and be careful not to read more into questions than is actually there.

8. Deliberately ignore the pace of classmates and proceed with a steady pace.

9. Draw mind maps or create outlines on the back of the test for future reference. Use them as a "starting point."

10. Answer all questions. Use intelligent guessing strategies for those you don't know — flag those questions and come back to them to recheck your answers. (Be sure to find out if there is a penalty for guessing.)

11. Never change an answer unless it is *clearly* wrong.

12. Your subconscious will continue to "work" on questions about which you are unsure. Sometimes a question/answer will trigger recall for another question/answer.

13. If you get "stuck"...
- Reread the question and break it down into small units.
- Search for the "cue" or "clue" words and define them mentally.
- Carefully reread the answer choices (read the stem first and then each answer with it — the stem is the "question" above the answers).
- Put yourself in your teacher's position and try to determine what he or she wants.
- Try to recall particular phrases the teacher might have repeated/related to the idea/concept.
- Visualize the event, time line, section of the book, etc., in which the answer might be found.
- Brainstorm associated concepts and try to recall similar information.
- Put the question into your own words for better understanding, being very careful not to change the meaning.
- Draw a picture or diagram to really "see" it.

14. Check your answers.
- Are they readable?
- Do they answer the questions asked?
- Are they in the correct answer spaces?
- Have they been transposed correctly from "workspace?"
- Have they been written well (if an essay)?

I. **MULTIPLE-CHOICE TEST STRATEGIES:**

A. **They are the tests most often given by teachers.**

B. **You are asked to recognize related information.**

C. **Understand the directions.**
    1. Read all directions twice.
    2. Is there one or more than one correct answer per question?

D. **Work quickly.**

E. **"Flag" questions about which you are unsure and continue.**

F. **Answer the question (never leave a blank unless you are penalized for unanswered questions).**

    1. Study the stem (the "question" above the choices) and circle any qualifiers or key words (refer to "List of 'Qualifiers'" — page 189).

    2. Guess the answer before reading the choices.

    3. Separate the questions or answers into smaller parts if you find them complicated or confusing.

4. Read all of the choices before making a decision.

5. Eliminate obviously wrong answers.

   a. Refer to "Intelligent Guessing Strategies" — page 191).

   b. Look for "clue" words or numbers.

   c. Watch for grammatical clues.

      1) Noun/verb agreement between stem and answer

      2) A/an in stem — answer begins with vowel

      3) Plurals

   d. Be on the lookout for familiar phrases from lectures or the text.

6. When you get stuck, try reading the stem with each possible answer (separately).

G. If time permits, recheck your answers.

   1. Look for flagged questions first.

   2. Before changing any answers, be sure you have a very good reason to do so — your first response is usually correct.

I. TRUE/FALSE TEST STRATEGIES:

A. This kind of test is the most difficult to take.

B. You are asked to recognize specific facts and details.

C. Be sure you understand the directions.

1. Read all of the directions twice.

2. Look to see if there is a given number of true or false statements.

   a. Hint: There usually are more true answers than false answers because they are easier to write.

   b. If you must guess, answer true because the odds are better.

D. Read carefully.

1. Do *not* analyze each question for deeper meaning.

2. If the question is confusing, break it in half and thoroughly understand each part.

3. Look at the question from the test-maker's point of view.

4. Watch for "qualifying" words:

– because	– generally
– no one	– some
– nobody	– never
– only	– all wrong/right
– all	– always
– never	– none

(Refer to "List of 'Qualifiers'" for more words — page 189.)

E. Answer the question.

1. Always answer the questions about which you are unsure. Then, flag each question for a quick review.

2. You may not have time to come back to the question — any answer is better than nothing (if there is no penalty for guessing).

3. Find out before the test if there is a penalty for guessing.

4. Statements with "reasons" tend to be false (because they are incorrect or incomplete reasons).

5. Don't change your answers.

   a. Research shows that first answers usually are correct.

   b. Be absolutely sure before changing an answer.

6. Assume that the statement is true unless you determine it to be false.

   a. It's easier to write true statements than to make false statements seem true.

   b. All parts of a true/false question must be true before it can be true.

7. Cross out all pairs of negatives and then reread the question.

I. MATCHING TEST STRATEGIES:

A. You are asked to recognize specific facts and details.

B. Understand the directions well. Find out if each answer is used once or more than once.

C. Read both columns before starting (read the longest column first).

D. Choose the longest column and work down that one first.

1. This column has more clues and more information.

2. Cross off used answers as you go.

3. Do the easiest matches first.

4. Match tough ones last through the process of elimination.

E. If you're stumped:

1. Try to recall where (in text or notes) you remember seeing this item.

   a. This will help you to associate the item with a main idea or concept.

   b. Perhaps you will "see" the heading on the page.

FILL-IN-THE-BLANK TESTS

I. FILL-IN-THE-BLANK TEST STRATEGIES:

A. You are asked to provide specific facts and details.

B. Understand the directions well and note if the responses are listed on another page or at the bottom of the questions page.

C. Read the question carefully and look for clue words (especially just before the blanks).

1. a, an, the, these, those, they
2. Clue words indicate vowel/consonant, singular/plural words.
3. Often they appear after the blank.

D. Answer the question.

1. Write/print clearly.
2. Be sure your answer "fits" the question.
3. Sometimes the teacher uses sentences taken from the text.

E. When you're stuck:

1. Brainstorm for a moment.
2. If you can't think of the exact word, write a synonym or definition for that word or phrase. Partial credit is better than none.
3. Write all possible answers. Flag the question and come back to it. Your mind will continue to think and possibly will recall the answer later.
4. Try to picture the concept at a certain place in your notes and/or text. Associate this with the concept.

I. NUMBER TEST STRATEGIES:

A. You are asked to provide reasons, proof and specific answers.

B. Understand the directions well. The directions usually ask you to cite rules or formulas and to apply these in order to arrive at a specific answer.

C. Write clearly.
1. Be sure each number is recognizable.
2. Keep numbers in proper columns or the spaces provided.

D. Copy the problem correctly.
1. Make sure you have copied the problem correctly before working it.
2. Have in mind the correct answer label if one is required.
3. If answer columns are used, double-check the answer as you transfer it from the workspace.

E. Estimate the answer first.
1. Get a "ballpark" answer in mind.
2. For multiple-choice questions, work the problem before looking at the answers.

F. Watch for measurement units.
1. Be sure to convert properly if necessary.
2. Label your answer correctly.

G. Watch for "dead wood" numbers. Cross out unnecessary given facts/ numbers that have been thrown in to cause confusion.

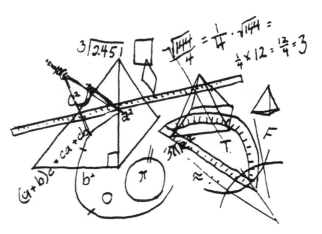

H. Check the arithmetic of all problems.

1. Check even the simplest addition and subtraction steps.

2. Most wrong answers are due to arithmetic errors.

I. When you get stuck:

1. Watch for clue words such as *additional, equally, less,* etc.

2. Illustrate the problem by drawing a picture, diagram or graph.

3. Reread the question by breaking it down into simple parts.

4. Change complicated and complex numbers into whole numbers and try to work the problem as an example.

5. Make an educated guess when all else fails (*if* you will not be penalized for guessing).

    a. Eliminate unusual fractions and measurements.

    b. Eliminate the highest and lowest answers in multiple-choice questions.

I. ESSAY TEST STRATEGIES:

A. Prepare before the test.

1. Anticipate test questions.
   a. Color-code class and text notes if possible.
   b. Make note of how much time the instructor devoted to each concept. The longer the time emphasis, the more probability there will be a question or two about this concept on the test.
   c. Be sure to study definitions and lists.
   d. Pay attention to handouts, study guides and review materials from the teacher.

2. **Map out answers.**
   a. For each question that you think will be on the test:
      1) Construct a brief outline (refer to "Essay Answer Format" — page 214).
      2) Make a graphic organizer/mind map.
   b. Be sure to include the following:
      1) All main ideas and supporting details
      2) Details and examples
      3) Key words/phrases (check spelling)
      4) Relationships/connections with other concepts stressed in class
   c. Memorize your mind map/outline.

B. Three main ingredients of an essay:

1. Knowledge of the subject
2. Organization of ideas
3. Writing skills

C. Find out in advance who is grading the essays and promote ideas that appeal to the grader.

D. During the test:

1. Read all of the questions before you begin.

   a. Note how many points each essay question is worth and start with the one that is worth the most points.

   b. Jot down a few phrases about each question as you read through the test.

      1) This helps when you want to begin writing.

      2) It jogs your memory.

   c. Reading all of the questions will keep you from repeating information.

2. Decide on a time limit for each question.

   a. Go to the next question if your time runs out.

   b. Four partially answered questions will give you more credit than two completed questions and two blank questions.

   c. Budget your time for each question.

      1) 50% outlining

      2) 50% writing

   d. Write your time estimates in the margin.

3. Reread the directions.

4. Reread the question and circle important words concerning *what* and *how* to write the answer (refer to "Essay Direction Words" — page 211).

5. Always organize your essay by making an outline.

6. Write methodically.

    a. Get involved with your answer — express your emotion.

    b. Leave a space between lines, if possible, so that you can add more information later if you choose.

    c. Define any terms you use.

    d. Use concrete examples.

    e. Introduction:
       1) Begin by restating the question in your own words.
       2) Establish tone and attitude.
       3) Be sure all following sentences relate to the topic sentence.

    f. Body:

       1) Use transitional words or statements.

       2) State main ideas clearly.

       3) Reinforce these ideas with supporting details.

       4) Support the details with examples whenever possible.

       5) Be sure to stay on track with the topic — answer the question.

    g. Conclusion:

       1) Use a summary sentence.

       2) Restate the main idea and point of view, but do not use examples.

       3) State how you proved, supported or defended your original idea.

7. Check your work.

    a. First, check for content.

       1) Answer the key words directly and precisely.

       2) Stick to your main point of view.

       3) Include enough details to support a clear statement.

    b. Secondly, check for organization. (Everything should tie together closely.)

        1) Introduction

        2) Body

        3) Conclusion

    c. Thirdly, check for mechanics.

        1) Omitted words

        2) Spelling errors

        3) Grammar

        4) Punctuation

        5) Awkward phrasing

        6) Use transitional statements to move smoothly from one paragraph to another, such as *first, second, third, then, however, finally,* etc.

8. Be sure to express what you really mean to say.

    a. Be concise — don't ramble.

    b. Be certain to answer the question.

    c. Demonstrate relationships between/among main points.

    d. Include examples whenever possible and appropriate.

    e. If in doubt, let your answer be more general than specific. (e.g. "In the 1920s…" rather than "In 1923… ")

    f. Use the asterisk system to add additional information when enough space has not been left.

9. If you run out of time, write "This is where I ran out of time" on your paper and include your outline.

10. What to do if you don't know the answer/topic:

    a. Look for "overlap" in what you do know.

    b. Look for ambiguous questions.

    c. Try to find relationships between what you studied and the question.

ESSAY DIRECTION WORDS

IF YOU ARE ASKED TO:	YOU SHOULD DO THE FOLLOWING:	EXAMPLES:
Analyze	Break down or separate a problem or situation into separate factors and/or relationships. Draw a conclusion, make a judgment, or make clear the relationship you see based on your breakdown.	Analyze the main story line in Chapter 2 and how it sets the stage for Chapter 3.
Categorize	Place items under headings already labeled by your teacher.	Categorize the items on the left under the proper headings on the right.
Classify	Place items in related groups; then name or title each group.	Listed below are 20 items. Classify them in 4 main groups; then name each group.
Compare	Tell how things are alike; use concrete examples.	Compare the American government system with that of the German government.
Contrast	Tell how things are different; use supporting concrete examples.	Contrast the writing styles of Shakespeare and Bacon.
Criticize	Make a judgment of the work of art or literature and support your judgment.	Criticize the use of cigarette advertising in magazines.
Deduce	Trace the course; derive a conclusion by reasoning.	Deduce the following logic problem to arrive at one of the conclusions listed below...
Defend	Give enough details to prove the statement.	Defend the statement "innocent until proven guilty."
Define	Give the meaning.	Define plankton.
Describe	Give an account in words; trace the outline or present a picture.	Describe Grand Coulee Dam.

From *Senior High Study Skills Booklet*, Jefferson County Schools, Colorado, © 1983. Used by permission.
© 1990 by Incentive Publications, Inc., Nashville, TN.

ESSAY DIRECTION WORDS *continued*

IF YOU ARE ASKED TO:	YOU SHOULD DO THE FOLLOWING:	EXAMPLES:
Diagram	Use pictures, graphs, charts mind maps & flow charts to show relationships of details to main ideas.	Diagram the offices of the federal government.
Discuss	Consider the various points of view by presenting all sides of the issue.	Discuss the use of chemotherapy in the treatment of cancer.
Distinguish	Tell how this is different from others similar to it.	Distinguish the three types of mold we have studied in class.
Enumerate	List all possible items.	Enumerate the presidents of the United States since Lincoln.
Evaluate	Make a judgment based on the evidence and support it; give the good and bad points.	Evaluate the use of pesticides.
Explain	Make clear and plain; give the reason or cause.	Explain how a natural disaster can help man.
Illustrate	Give examples, pictures, charts, diagrams or concrete examples to clarify your answer.	Illustrate the use of a drawbridge.
Interpret	Express your thinking by giving the meaning as you see it.	Interpret the line "Water, water everywhere and not a drop to drink."
Justify	Give some evidence by supporting your statement with facts.	Justify the decision to bomb Nagasaki, Japan.
List	Write in a numbered fashion.	List 5 reasons to support your statement.
Outline	Use a specific and shortened form to organize main ideas supporting details and examples.	Outline the leading cause of World War II.

From *Senior High Study Skills Booklet*, Jefferson County Schools, Colorado, © 1983. Used by permission.

ESSAY DIRECTION WORDS *continued*

IF YOU ARE ASKED TO:	YOU SHOULD DO THE FOLLOWING:	EXAMPLES:
Paraphrase	Put in your own words.	Paraphrase the first paragraph of the Gettysburg Address.
Predict	Present solutions that could happen if certain variables were present.	Predict the ending of the short story written below.
Prove	Provide factual evidence to back up the truth of the statement.	Prove that the whaling industry has led to almost extinction of certain varieties.
Relate	Show the relationship among concepts.	Relate man's survival instincts to those of animals.
Review	Examine the information critically. Analyze and comment on the important statements.	Review the effects of television advertisements on the public.
State	Establish by specifying. Write what you believe and back it with evidence.	State your beliefs in the democratic system of government.
Summarize	Condense the main points in the fewest words possible.	Summarize early man's methods of self-defense.
Synthesize	Combine parts or pieces of an idea, situation or event.	Synthesize the events leading up to the Civil War.
Trace	Describe in steps the progression of something.	Trace the importance of the prairie schooner to the opening of the West.
Verify	Confirm or establish the truth of accuracy of point of view with supporting examples, evidence and facts.	Verify the Declaration of Independence.

From *Senior High Study Skills Booklet*, Jefferson County Schools, Colorado, © 1983. Used by permission.
© 1990 by Incentive Publications, Inc., Nashville, TN.

Essay Answer Format

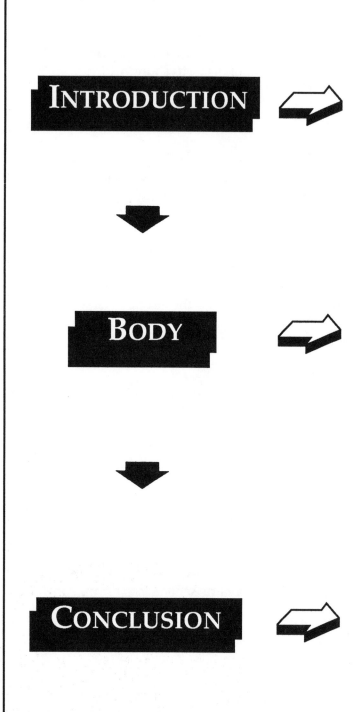

INTRODUCTION

Clearly state the main points.

Change the original question to a statement and include the main points.

BODY

Each paragraph should include:

- transitional word or statement
- main ideas
  - supporting details
  - examples

Be sure these points directly relate to the question and the topic in the introduction.

CONCLUSION

Begin with a good summary statement.

Include the main points covered in the body.

State how you proved, supported or defended your original intent in the introduction.

I. **OPEN-BOOK TEST STRATEGIES:**

A. **Be prepared.**

 1. Bring the following (be sure to clear all materials with the instructor before the date):

 a. Writing utensils (erasable ink pen, 2 - 3 pencils with erasers)

 b. Plenty of paper (lined and unlined, scratch paper)

 c. Texts

 d. Class notes

 e. Reading notes

 f. Study sheets, mind maps, outlines, graphic organizers

 g. 3" x 5" cards

B. **Know your textbook.**

 1. Be very familiar with:

 a. Table of contents

 b. Index

 c. Special appendixes

 d. Lists, charts, graphs, tables, summaries

 e. Author's intent in presentation of the material

 2. Read the chapters to be tested.

 a. Know the content.

 b. Know where to find associated information in other chapters.

C. **Make a special study guide several days in advance.**

1. Anticipate test questions and group all associated information together with page numbers (color-coding is very effective).

2. Save yourself valuable test-taking time by constructing:

   a. Lists of vocabulary words (check the spelling)

   b. Brief outlines for essay questions

   c. Graphic organizers of major concepts with supporting ideas and examples

   d. Your own concept index with page numbers from your notes and text (remember to number your notes and all other papers)

D. **When you get the test:**

1. Scan the test quickly and look for a format (T/F, multiple-choice, fill-in-the-blank, matching, essay questions).

2. Plan your "attack."

   a. Organize your time appropriately.

      1) Notice which sections are worth the most points.

      2) Notice which sections seem to be related according to subject area.

      3) Essay questions take more time — plan for this.

   b. Read and then reread *all* directions carefully.

I. TAKE-HOME TEST STRATEGIES:

A. You are asked to research, organize and combine information.

B. Before you leave class:

1. Scan the entire test and ask any questions you might have.

2. Be sure that you understand all directions.

3. List all references/materials to be used. (When in doubt, ask the teacher.)

4. Be very clear about the due date and time.

5. Find out if this is an individual or group effort.

6. Ask about any restrictions.

7. Find out the expected length for answers if essay questions are involved.

C. At home:

1. Gather any/all needed materials.

   a. Textbook

   b. Class notes, reading notes, notes from outside assignments

   c. Dictionary

   d. Thesaurus

   e. Study sheets, 3" x 5" cards

   f. Writing utensils
      (pens/pencils/erasers)

   g. Basic English grammar
      reference

2. Plan your time allotment for each part of the test according to its point value — begin with the most valuable part.

3. Read the entire test.

    a. Read all directions very carefully.

    b. Look for related questions and answers throughout the test.

    c. Circle or flag qualifiers (words).

    d. Try to understand the overall objectives of the test and what the teacher wants from you.

4. Plan and organize your answers.

    a. Refer to specific test strategies in this section.

    b. Double-check all objective test answers.

    c. Be sure all essay answers are well-written.

    d. Make a list of the references you use and attach it to your test.

        1) Don't copy directly from any source.

        2) If you do use quotes, be sure to use the proper punctuation and identification.

5. If you have time, write a first draft and then recopy it, proofreading for spelling, punctuation, content, grammar, organization and clarity.

6. Staple all papers together before handing in the test.

7. Be sure your name is on every page of the test.

Watch What You're Doing!

LISTEN	for oral directions
LOOK	over the entire test
WRITE	brief notes; draw mind maps
BUDGET	time to allow for completion
READ	directions twice; circle key words
ANSWER	questions; known first, unknown second
CHECK	all answers

After the Test

I. **REVIEW YOUR RETURNED TEST**

   A. **Why? To avoid repeated mistakes.**

   B. **Read all of the grader's comments.**
     1. Turn any criticism into a useful tool for future reference.
     2. Learn from your mistakes — take a positive viewpoint.
     3. Make a mental note of the positive comments and try to repeat these achievements.

   C. **Look for specifics.**
     1. Note what types of questions you answer well.
     2. Note what types of questions are your weakest; review test-taking strategies for these types of questions.
     3. Was important information missing from your class notes or study sheets?
     a. Why was it missing?
     b. Was it recorded incorrectly?
     c. What can you do in the future to correct this?
     4. Did you allow yourself enough time for each part of the test, or will you have to budget your time differently for the next test?
     5. What amount of the test was covered in class notes, outside reading assignments and class discussion periods?

   D. **Pay attention to class discussion of the test.**
     1. Write on test improvements you could have made.
     2. Correct the wrong answers — write better answers.

   E. **Keep all tests in a file for future reference.**

II. **IF YOU DID POORLY ON THE TEST, GET HELP FROM:**

   A. **Teacher(s)**

   B. **Family**

   C. **Friends**

   D. **Tutor(s)**

ETC.

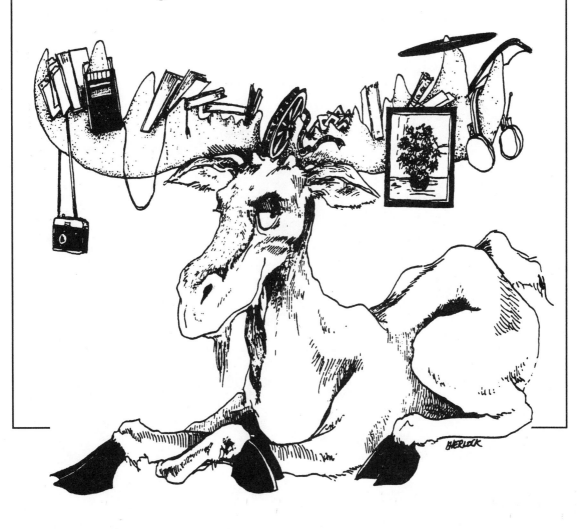

FOCUS ON

ETC.

1. With anything you learn, always: Hear It, See It, Say It, Write It and Do It.

2. Use your thinking skills effectively.

3. Practice problem-solving steps.

4. Be prepared for teacher conferences.

5. Utilize questioning and context clues to your advantage.

6. Apply a spelling system that really works.

7. Use and organize plan of attack for independent study projects.

8. Apply divergent thinking characteristics to your learning.

9. Strive to use higher level thinking skills to relate information.

10. Learn how to learn to make the most efficient use of your time.

IMPROVE YOUR THINKING SKILLS

To develop "successful" thinking skills you must gather information, take a new approach when necessary, and look at the whole picture from different angles. Thinking is a skill which can be improved with continual and deliberate effort. You have to intend to think through problem-solving strategies and open your mind to creativity.

These ideas will sharpen your thinking and increase your creative approach. Try some of them and you may be surprised by the wonderful results!

- **Learn to see the whole picture.**

    - Then break it down by looking at the details.

    - Consider your surroundings and what is happening.

- **Be flexible with your thinking.**

    - Brainstorm as many solutions/answers as you can.

    - Try an entirely new approach.

    - Write your ideas so that you can refer to them from day-to-day.

    - Spend some time with others who are trying to solve the problem.

- **Practice making decisions.**

    - Like most everything else, it becomes easier the more you do it.

    - Set your goals and think about what you want.

    - Observe the situation carefully — try to see things you have never noticed.

- **Be open to change.**

  - Try to have a positive mental attitude toward most changes.

  - See the positive side and what you can do to improve it for yourself and others.

  - Think of ways you can turn the negative aspects into positive aspects.

  - Remember that thinking can be wasted or improved.

- **Fold a piece of paper in half vertically:**

  - Place a + on the top of the left column.

  - Place a – on the top of the right column.

  - When approaching any difficult problem-solving task or decision, write all of the positive and negative aspects, no matter how trivial or foolish they may seem to you.

  - Compare the columns and THINK, then ACT.

PROBLEM-SOLVING

A teacher is more than a person who stands in front of the classroom and imparts knowledge. How wonderful it would be for students if teachers could open up the tops of their students' heads and pour precious bits of ideas and details into every nook and cranny! But there is much more to teaching than that.

Teachers like to share what they have learned through books and experiences. They want their students to understand the concepts they teach. Throughout the learning experience, teachers not only encourage their students to apply what they have learned, but they motivate their students to reason, think, question and relate the material to other information so that it makes sense.

It's good to focus your thoughts on what teachers try to do. It's so easy to over-look a teacher's good qualities when you're having trouble in his or her class and/or you personally do not like the teacher. If you stop to think about it, you definitely learn better from teachers you like and enjoy. But what about those instructors who share their course content in a way that is less than enjoyable to you? What can you do if you really do not like a teacher or find it difficult to relate to a teacher? Just remember that teachers are people, too. Besides, if you can learn some important "people skills," life will be a lot easier for you!

Give some serious thought to the "Problem Areas And Suggestions" on pages 227 and 228. One of the problems might be something that you currently are facing. If so, try some of the positive solutions. Remember, you have to TRY!

STEP 1

Face it — YOU have the problem.

Even if you think it is entirely the other person's fault (the teacher), you have a problem because the "problem" bothers you. Take ownership of the problem.

 STEP 2

Try to identify the problem.

Determine what it is that bothers or disturbs you. Is it really the person or what the person does? If you can see the problem for what it is, you can begin to look for the solution(s).

 STEP 3

Look at your options.

You can continue to waste negative energy on the problem and let it interfere with learning, or you can give yourself permission to dislike (or even hate) the problem and then refocus your energies on a positive path. Walking down the "positive path" allows you to pick up what you need — you feel more at ease with yourself. Running down the "negative path" only serves to wear you down — you won't have the opportunity to pick up anything along the way. Say this to yourself: "I don't like this and that's OK. Now, what can I do to get what I want or need?" In other words, "I don't like this class/teacher and that's OK. Now, what can I do to learn the information and get the grade I want?"

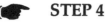 **STEP 4**

Think of several solutions.

Be practical, realistic and serious. Will these solutions really work? Can I give each solution an honest try? Write the solutions on a piece of paper, and if time permits, give yourself time to think about them. Dedicate yourself to putting one or more solutions into practice.

STEP 5

Put your solution(s) into practice.

Begin with a positive attitude. You've thought through your solution(s) step-by-step and now you have enough self-confidence to start your "plan of attack." Think of it as a learning experience — you'll know so much if you should have to face this same problem in the future! If your approach to people is positive, your efforts will reflect positively on you. If your solution doesn't work to your satisfaction, try another solution — but don't quit! You have everything to gain and nothing to lose.

Suppose you have a problem (misunderstanding, lack of understanding, question or need help) with a class or teacher and you don't know quite how to approach the teacher. It's really easier to solve than you might think. Follow these simple rules and you'll enjoy success!

1. Know what you want to ask or discuss. Write it on paper if necessary.

2. Rehearse your approach and questions/statements mentally or orally.

3. Find a time when the teacher is not busy with students or other teachers and is not in a hurry. A time when he/she can devote some focused attention to your conversation is best. Set up an appointment if necessary.

4. Arrive a minute or two early or arrange to stay after class if necessary.

5. Begin with a positive statement and then simply state what you want or need.

    Example: "I'm sincerely interested in learning the information your class (lab, lecture, etc.) offers. But, lately I'm having a hard time understanding and keeping up, and I'd like to know what I can do to help myself."

6. Actively listen (and take notes if you feel the need) to what the teacher says and/or suggests. Thank the instructor for his or her time and assure him or her that you will try to put the suggestions into practice.

7. Tell the teacher that you will get in touch with him or her in two weeks (or the appropriate time) to share the improvements or to ask for further assistance.

8. Find ways to demonstrate your interest in class. Take part in discussions, ask thoughtful questions, and try to use some of the suggestions/ideas the teacher related to you during your conference, etc.

9. MOST OF ALL...be positive, courteous, considerate, willing to see the other side, and willing to try!

CRITICAL BRAIN POWER SKILLS

READING	WRITING	THINKING
determining purpose	fluency	recall/memory
determining rate	writing legibly	understanding concepts
effective note-taking	spelling	visualization
recognizing signals	note-taking	understanding organizational patterns
surveying material	clear, organized expression	critical thinking
developing a system	creativity	brainstorming
questioning	editing notes	classifying
reciting	proofreading	relaxation
reviewing	self-expression	
determining main ideas	reading	
intent to remember	creativity	
predicting	positive thinking	
reading charts	mind set of intentional learning	
comprehension	summarizing	
vocabulary development	relating & transferring concepts	
fluency	understanding relationships between main ideas & supporting details	
writing	evaluating	
	curiosity	

CRITICAL BRAIN POWER SKILLS *continued*

CLASSROOM SKILLS	PERSONAL ATTRIBUTES	TEST-TAKING SKILLS
active listening	curiosity	organizing information
note-taking, writing	serious intent to learn	recognizing anxiety
speaking (relating ideas clearly)	patience	recall/memory
	knowledge of learning style	practice
brainstorming	risk-taking	overlearning
discussion skills	thinking with an open mind	scheduling
test-taking skills		testwiseness
completing homework	organizing	organizing
organizing assignments & notebooks	prioritizing	positive attitude
classifying	willing to practice	concentrating
locating information quickly	goal-setting	focusing thinking
relating concepts	positive thinking	
questioning	perseverance	
reading flexibility	understanding of confusion & boredom	
focusing concentration		
demonstrating interest	flexibility	
showing respect	realistic & constructive use of time	
patience		
understanding directions		
knowledge of self-commitment		
independence		

THINKING . . . ODDS AND ENDS

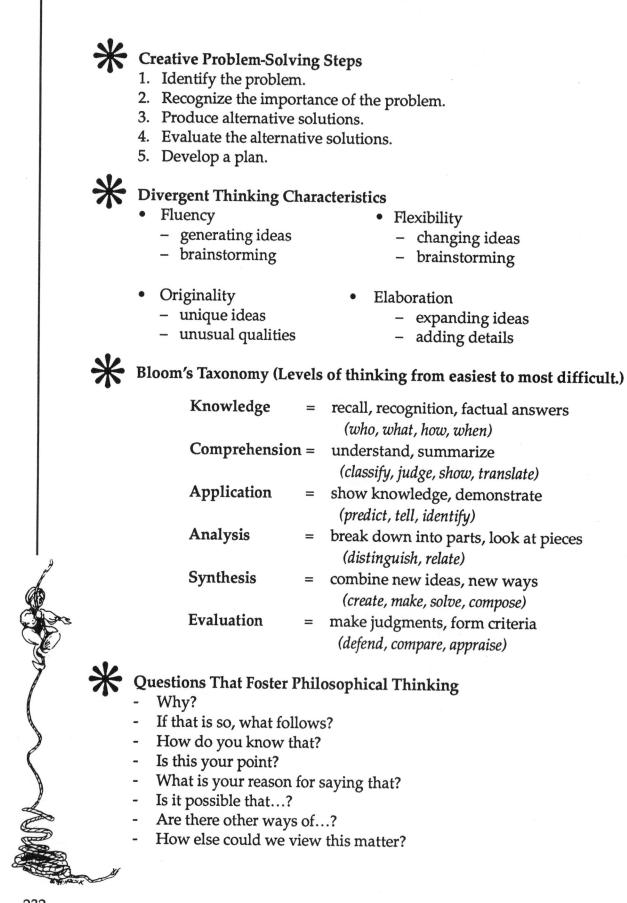

✳ **Creative Problem-Solving Steps**
1. Identify the problem.
2. Recognize the importance of the problem.
3. Produce alternative solutions.
4. Evaluate the alternative solutions.
5. Develop a plan.

✳ **Divergent Thinking Characteristics**

- Fluency
  - generating ideas
  - brainstorming

- Flexibility
  - changing ideas
  - brainstorming

- Originality
  - unique ideas
  - unusual qualities

- Elaboration
  - expanding ideas
  - adding details

✳ **Bloom's Taxonomy (Levels of thinking from easiest to most difficult.)**

Knowledge = recall, recognition, factual answers
(who, what, how, when)

Comprehension = understand, summarize
(classify, judge, show, translate)

Application = show knowledge, demonstrate
(predict, tell, identify)

Analysis = break down into parts, look at pieces
(distinguish, relate)

Synthesis = combine new ideas, new ways
(create, make, solve, compose)

Evaluation = make judgments, form criteria
(defend, compare, appraise)

✳ **Questions That Foster Philosophical Thinking**
- Why?
- If that is so, what follows?
- How do you know that?
- Is this your point?
- What is your reason for saying that?
- Is it possible that...?
- Are there other ways of...?
- How else could we view this matter?

What anyone needs to do to think:
- Communicate information with/to someone else through writing or conversation.
- Experiment.
- Constantly review, evaluate and analyze the information.
- Conceptualize and link new ideas/information with old ideas/information.
- Interpret information through inductive and deductive thinking.
- Exercise flexible thinking.

 In order to learn anything:
1. Link it with something you already know; develop a strategy for learning (mnemonics).
2. Understand and use what you're trying to learn; use/practice the strategy.
3. Understand how/why you will apply this information in your future; apply the strategy to other learning.
4. Integrate your knowledge of *how* and *why* you learn with *what* you learn.

Good study/review questions:
- Can you briefly summarize what you just read? What/Who was important and why?
- Can you explain your answer?
- Can you state examples and tell why are they are important?
- Do you agree? Why or why not?
- How did you arrive at your answer or solution? What are your "thinking" steps?
- What facts support your view and can you think of others not stated?
- Can you apply these ideas to other situations or information?
- Can you add information to this subject or compare and contrast it with what you already know?

CLUES AND ANSWERS

FOUR TYPES OF CONTEXT CLUES:

1. **Definition** – the easiest to use ("is, means…")

2. **Comparison** – unknown words compared with know words ("as, like…")

3. **Contrast** – opposite meaning ("but, not, however…")

4. **Sense of Passage** – think about the meaning in relation to other parts of the paragraph

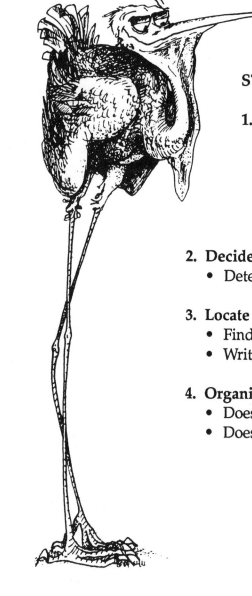

STEPS IN ANSWERING A QUESTION:

1. **Read**
   - Read the question carefully.
   - What is the question asking you?
   - Do you know the meaning of all the words?
   - Underline the key words.

2. **Decide**
   - Determine if it is a factual or thought question.

3. **Locate**
   - Find information relating to the question.
   - Write the information in your own words.

4. **Organize**
   - Does your answer make sense?
   - Does it answer the question?

STEP 1   **Study the words for two to three minutes (approximately 20 words).**
- Concentrate — focus on each word.
  - double letters (bookkeeper)
  - words within words (tremendous)
  - letter patterns (interpret)
  - exceptions to spelling rules
  - able/ible endings
  - er/or endings
  - compound words
- Make quick mental pictures.
- Think of nonsense sayings.

STEP 2   **Take a trial test.**
- Have someone say the words to you (in a sentence if possible).
- Write the words.

STEP 3   **Correct the trial test.**
- Say the word.
- Have the person spell the word while you write it beside your spelling.
- Check the two words for a match.

STEP 4   **Rewrite the incorrect words.**
- Write each word on a separate 3" x 5" card.
- As you write, orally repeat each letter.

STEP 5   **Write all of the words on one 3" x 5" card.**

STEP 6   **Retake the trial test.**
- Correct yourself by checking the words against the 3" x 5" card.
- Orally spell each word as you check the card.

STEP 7   **Post 3" x 5" cards where they can be seen every day.**
- your room, bulletin board, mirror, etc. (in upper left corner)
- locker door (at school)
- refrigerator door
- in a notebook or book (Use them when standing in the lunch line or when waiting for class to begin.)

How To Help At Home

- Put a priority on reading and demonstrate it!

- Show your enthusiasm for education by taking an active interest in your child's schooling.

- Attend school functions.

- Have a conference with your child's teacher.

- Make a point to talk *with* (not at) your child about daily activities.

- Provide an adequate breakfast and lunch for your child.

- Talk about teachers in a positive tone in front of your child.

- Encourage your child to participate in the "extras" the school offers.

- Know what classes and assignments your child has.

- Become familiar with late homework/make-up policies.

- Find out when/if teachers are available for extra help.

- Monitor the number of hours your child watches/uses television, video games, etc.

- Help your child establish good time management techniques and check on this from time to time.

- Encourage your child to learn how to learn.

- Discuss your child's intent to learn with him or her.

- Know how your child learns best and take advantage of this information.

- Try to discuss the day's activities around the dinner table.

Plan of Attack for Independent Study

STEP 1 – SELECT A TOPIC.

- Look through books and resource materials.
- Brainstorm for ideas with family and friends.
- Follow your own interests or hobbies.
- Interview others.
- Read the newspaper or a current magazine.
- Watch the news on T V.

STEP 2 – NARROW THE TOPIC.

- Limit the topic and consider the following: desired length, amount of in-class and out-of-class time needed, your access to resources, your time schedule.
- Narrow the topic enough so that you may cover it thoroughly, but not so narrow that there won't be enough available information.
- Form definite questions you want to answer. Avoid yes/no, one-word and short-phrase answers.

STEP 3 – PUT YOUR TOPIC TO THE TEST.

- How much information can you actually locate to answer the questions?
- Is the material easy to find in the media center, from resource people, etc? Can you take the material home?
- Can you complete the project by the due date?

STEP 4 – CHOOSE YOUR RESOURCES.

- Books, pamphlets, magazines
- T V, films, filmstrips, videotapes, movies
- People (interviews, polls, questionnaires)
- Travel
- Illustrated graphics (charts, graphs, tables, pictures)
- Experiment — use your senses.

STEP 5 — SCHEDULE YOUR TIME.

- Divide your time into realistic blocks. Consider the following:
  - Library/media center check-out time periods–Postal service (if you're sending for material)
  - Actual contact time with people (and time to make arrangements)
  - In-class and homework time
  - Basic outline, rough draft, illustrations, front cover and other steps in organizing the report/project

STEP 6 — BEGIN YOUR RESEARCH.

- Begin at the media center.
  - Look for information related to your topic in the following areas:
    - Card catalog
    - Reader's guide
    - Reference section
    - Almanacs, maps
    - Visual center (filmstrips, cassettes, tapes, films, etc.)
  - Keep a "running list" of titles, authors, publishers, and page numbers of every source you use (also note the call number or location beside each item).
- Skim through the material before writing anything. This saves time and energy.
- Stay organized.
  - Keep everything related to the project in a notebook, box, filing card system, etc.
  - Organize a notebook and section off the different aspects of the topic/report.
- Ask the librarian or your teacher any questions concerning resources (the media specialist just might know of a resource you overlooked).
- The more variety of materials you can collect, the better (if they are appropriate to the project).

STEP 7 — ORGANIZE AND PRESENT YOUR PROJECT.

- Be creative.
    - Think of unusual ways to present your material/information (when the assignment allows it).
    - Slide shows
    - Live interviews
    - News broadcasts
    - Videotapes
    - Radio programs
    - Inventions with explanations
    - Puzzles or games (involve other students)
    - Computer graphics
    - Pamphlets or brochures
    - Murals
    - Three-dimensional models or exhibits
    - Puppet plays
    - Oral presentations (dress in costume)
    - Speeches or testimonials (dress in costume)
- Be sure to:
    - Rehearse before you give the presentation.
    - Check all of the materials for proper order.
    - Complete the assignment a day or so before it is due to allow for the addition of any last minute details and to let yourself relax.
    - Recheck the original assignment to make sure your project/report satisfies all of the conditions or answers all of the questions and criteria.

ACKNOWLEDGEMENTS

Beffie, Daryl. "Clues And Answers" (page 234). Reprinted by permission.

CMU Junior League. "Time Management" (page 32), "What To Do If You Missed An Assignment" (page 43): from *The Campus Cache: A Cookbook For Study Skills*, © 1982 by Cherry Creek School District. Reprinted by permission.

Isakson, Peggy. "Power Reading System" (pages 132-135). Reprinted by permission.

Jefferson County Schools, Colorado. "Study Habits Inventory" (pages 34-36), "Organizing Your Assignments" (pages 39-40), "Activities In Taking Classroom Notes" (pages 72-73), "Terms For Taking Notes" (page 74), "Surveying The Textbook" (pages 127-128), "Essay Direction Words" (pages 211-213): adapted from *Senior High Study Skills Booklet*, © 1983. Reprinted by permission.

Piccolo, JoAnne. *Enumerative, Sequence, Cause-Effect, Comparison-Contrast, & Description Graphic Organizers* (pages 110-114). Reprinted by permission.